Penrhyn Castle

Gwynedd

Ymddiriedolaeth Genedlaethol
National Trust

Built to impress

Penrhyn is perhaps the most extraordinary fantasy castle built in Britain in the 19th century. But this is no fairytale. What was created here shaped thousands of lives – for good and ill – from North Wales to the West Indies.

An ancient site

Penrhyn Castle occupies a strategic position between two rivers on the route from England to Bangor and the isle of Anglesey. There has been a house on this site since medieval times, and fragments of it can still be glimpsed within the present building and in the garden.

A power house

Penrhyn may resemble a gigantic Norman castle, but it was constructed as recently as 1820–32 by the architect Thomas Hopper for George Hay Dawkins-Pennant. The castle can never have been very cosy or practical, but it has survived remarkably unchanged. It was intended to demonstrate in stone the colossal wealth and power of the Pennant family. Their money came originally from sugar plantations in Jamaica, which were established in the 17th century. The profits generated by the Pennants' slave workers in the Caribbean were invested back in North Wales, where Richard Pennant created and modernised a huge agricultural estate in the late 18th century. He also established a slate quarry at nearby Bethesda, which was at one time the largest in the world. The Pennants ran the quarry in a paternalistic but authoritarian fashion, which was increasingly resented by the quarrymen. The result was the famous strike of 1900–3, which has left a legacy of bitterness among the local people that has still not entirely disappeared.

Living in style

Not surprisingly, slate features prominently in the decoration of the castle's interiors, which were furnished with richly coloured stained glass, wallpapers and fabrics. Hopper designed furniture specially for Penrhyn in a complementary Norman style. Carving abounds throughout the castle, which testifies to the skills of local craftsmen. In the second half of the 19th century, Edward Gordon Douglas-Pennant assembled a distinguished collection of Dutch, Spanish and Italian Old Masters, most of which still hangs here, earning Penrhyn the title of the 'National Gallery of North Wales'. The family entertained on an equally grand scale, and created a complex network of kitchen quarters to cater for their banquets. The kitchens are shown today as they would have been arranged during the visit of the Prince of Wales in 1894. Distinguished guests were encouraged to plant trees in the garden, which provided a suitably grand setting for the castle.

Welcoming visitors

Penrhyn may look like a forbidding fortress, but visitors were being shown round even before it was finished. Lord Penrhyn built a tourist route and hotels nearby that sold admission tickets to the castle when the family was away, which was for much of the year. You are following in the footsteps of these early visitors.

So much to see

Penrhyn is not just a huge historic house with servants' quarters and garden on the same scale. The stable block offers museums devoted to dolls and railway engines and a varied programme of changing exhibitions. If you don't manage to see it all in one visit, please do come again soon. There is always more to enjoy.

(Left) The east front

(Right) Col. Edward Douglas-Pennant (in top hat) with family and visitors to Penrhyn in 1866

Tour of the Castle

The Entrance Gallery

The narrow, low Entrance Gallery gives the impression of a Norman cloister. It was clearly designed to accentuate the impact of the Grand Hall beyond, which is partly hidden from view by the offsetting of the doorways in between.

Furniture and metalwork

Along the Gallery and vestibule are several of Hopper's neo-Norman carved oak *tables and desks* made by the estate carpenters; early 18th-century Flemish armchairs with carved cherub heads to the arms; some 'ancient' *hall-chairs* probably made to Hopper's order and based on a late 16th-century German pattern book; and two oak *hall-chairs* with double-headed eagles carved in the oval backs and dated 1729 (probably made up in the 1830s by Hopper).

The most bizarre piece is a high-backed carved oak *armchair* whose eclectic composition epitomises early 19th-century antiquarian taste. The central panel of the back, surrounded by late 17th-century-style decoration, is carved with a standing figure of a crusader. The 'wings' seem indebted to a 'Renaissance' source, the seat and arms are covered in late 17th-century embossed leather, and the cabriole legs are of a basically Georgian kind.

The set of four bronzed iron *colza-oil lamps* on pedestals lost their oil reservoirs with the coming of electricity. Their wolf-heads may have been derived from the antique Capitoline Wolf bronze in Rome.

* denotes items accepted in lieu of Inheritance Tax

Lighting

The huge lamps were sculpted in the form of monstrous beasts from an unidentified ceramic successor of Coade stone. Their maker is not known.

The Grand Hall

The vast empty volume of the Grand Hall is as much a covered courtyard as a room. The floor here (and in the adjacent passages and stairs) is of York stone, specified by Hopper on the strength of its recent use at Westminster.

Pictures

The *portraits* are thought to be of Sir Samuel (1709–50) and John Pennant (d. 1781). *John the Baptist preaching to Herod** was painted in 1848 by John Rogers Herbert, a precursor of the Pre-Raphaelites.

Stained glass

The stained glass was all supplied in 1835–6 by Thomas Willement, who travelled from London in July 1834 'to see the situation of the Hall windows'. The two largest, at the northern end, are signed by him and dated 1835. They are among his best work, incorporating the signs of the zodiac alternating with roundels illustrating the months of the year.

Furniture

The large octagonal carved oak *tilt-top table** was designed by Hopper and incorporates fragments from earlier furniture in the pedestal base. His startlingly original oak *chairs*, with backs carved like the vanes of some marine organism, are surprisingly comfortable and give excellent support to the back. The *piano* is a Broadwood concert grand in a rosewood case, No. 47778, 1903. The *clock* above the fireplace is by William Johnson, '50 Strand, London, 1835', and the accompanying wind-direction dial is linked to a vane on the roof.

Textiles

The machine-woven Axminster 'Turkey' *runner* was made in 1987, reproducing the hand-knotted carpet in the Keep Passage, which is probably late 19th-century. The woollen velvet *curtains* date from the early 1830s.

The Grand Hall

The Library

The Library was intended not only as the evening resort of gentlemen, but as a setting for family entertainments. High Victorian Penrhyn obviously witnessed such productions: an inventory of 1928 lists 'Theatrical Equipment' among the croquet sets languishing in an upper passage. But the Library must chiefly be thought of as the gentlemen's domain, resembling as it does a London club.

Decoration

The room partly incorporates the area of the medieval house, and this may have suggested the historical emphasis of the decoration. The flattened form of the three main arches resembles that of the Norman chancel arch at Tickencote church, Leicestershire, which had been rebuilt in the 1790s and included in John Carter's *Ancient Architecture* of 1798. The decoration is almost unchanged since Hawkins's 1846 lithograph (illustrated on p. 7).

Stained glass

Probably the work of David Evans of Shrewsbury, who was paid £7 6s for stained glass in 1836, it shows the arms of the five 'royal' and fifteen 'noble' tribes of Wales, groupings first made at the end of the 15th century by the bards – with little reference to historical fact – and taken up by the 18th-century antiquaries.

Chimneypieces

The four chimneypieces are of polished Penmon limestone ('Penmon marble') laid down on Anglesey 345 million years ago. The capitals of one of them are carved with two friezes of mummers, taken from the marginalia of a 14th-century Bruges manuscript, as illustrated in Joseph Strutt's *Sports and Pastimes* (1801).

Books*

Most of the books date from the 18th and early 19th centuries. They are an attractive mixture of the impressive and the quite ordinary, and seem to have mostly been bought by the builder of the castle and his son-in-law. As it survives today, the collection has a good representation of topography, history, architecture and antiquities. The **bookcases** were designed by Hopper in the form of classical temples, but in a Norman style.

The *billiard-table* may originally have been in the Ebony Room. By 1943 it was at the southern end of the Grand Hall, and was moved to its present position in order to make room for the typing pool of the Daimler Co. Ltd. Unusually, not only the bed but the entire frame and legs and even the pockets are composed of enamelled slate, and its construction is also thought to be unique. It was made for Col. Edward Douglas-Pennant by George Eugene Magnus, who owned a quarry in North Wales and established the Pimlico Slate Works in London in 1840.

Furniture

The room contains a mixture of contemporary, 'ancient' and composite furniture. Contemporary are the *circular table* on a tripod stand, veneered in coromandel wood and inlaid with brass; the *pole-screens* with embroideries by Charlotte Douglas, sister of the 1st Lord Penrhyn; and the *seat furniture* upholstered in stamped wool velvets. These velvets were produced in the 1820s–50s in Britain and the Netherlands, on embossed rollers, the designs taken from 16th- and 17th-century Italian models. The *prie-dieu chair* is covered in a cut-velvet directly reproducing a 17th-century Italian design.

Those pieces which may have been bought as 'ancient' include the 18th-century *'Burgomaster' chair* * from the Dutch East Indies, of a type illustrated in Henry Shaw's *Specimens of Ancient Furniture* (1836) as 'of the time of William the Third'; the *triangular armchair* with an inlaid ivory coronet in the back, of the same origin and date; and the two 17th-century Italian *high-backed armchairs*.

(Right) The Library in 1846; lithograph by G. Hawkins

There are several pieces designed by Thomas Hopper and made by the estate carpenters. These are the 'Norman'-style *square tables* with four cluster-column legs, and the *octagonal table* near the Grand Hall doorway, which incorporates ancient carvings applied to the frieze and column support. The decoration of the *great table* at the far end of the Library is also made up from a combination of old carvings with modern work in the same style.

The Boulle-work *mantel clock* is by Henry Balthazar, Paris, *c.*1740. The base is a 19th-century addition.

Carpets

The carpets at Penrhyn are either luxurious Axminsters based on continental examples or splendid inventions (either by Hopper or Willement) in the Norman style. The Library carpets must surely be in their original positions, although their detail differs from that in the lithograph. They are hand-knotted and most probably made at the Axminster factory. The colours, now much faded, were originally yellow ochre, terracotta and brown.

Stuffed birds

The group of exotic birds displayed under a glass dome includes two Indian Rollers (*Coracias bengalensis*; the large birds shown as in flight), some African shrikes (*Lanarius*) and an African mangrove kingfisher (*Halcyon senegaloides*).

The Drawing Room

The Drawing Room was the domain of the ladies.

Decoration

By the 1930s the dazzling silk hangings, curtains and upholstery had probably perished to an extent that they had to be removed, and for much of the 20th century the walls were covered by a dull brown paint. Probably also in the 1930s, the ceiling was painted over in white and the carved woodwork was stripped of its polish.

Stained glass

The medieval hall had been the work of Gwilym ap Gruffydd II and his wife Joan, and Thomas Pennant tells us that their arms could be seen in the windows until 1764. As an echo of this arrangement, Dawkins-Pennant set up his own arms and those of Elizabeth Bouverie, his second wife, over the central window. This glass and the heraldic windows to either side are attributed to David Evans of Shrewsbury.

Chimneypiece

The chimneypiece is of serpentinite, an igneous rock properly called Mona Marble, and this colour occurs in Llanfechell and Llandyfrydiog on Anglesey.

Furniture

Below the mirrors at either end is a pair of highly individual *tables**. The one against the Library wall is made entirely of slate, carved exceptionally deeply for this material, and the top slab incorporates 'sample' squares of colourful stones, probably all from Anglesey: in the three larger panels are the two varieties of Mona

Marble, the red one as used in the chimney-piece, and the green from Holy Island. At the far end of the room, the stand of the other table has the same design of entwined fishes and serpents, but in carved and gilt wood. These tables were presumably designed by Hopper, but their makers are not known.

The massive Tudor-style *oak settee*, the carved oak *chairs* and the *smaller settee* (with ancient carving applied to the back and apron) were all designed by Hopper.

The *octagonal table* with marquetry in the frieze and tripod stand is by Edward Holmes Baldock. Baldock may also have 'made up' the oval table with an 'oyster' marquetry top on a

The Drawing Room

8

The gilt-bronze candelabra in the Drawing Room may have been made in Venice in the 1840s. The figures were inspired by Antique models

17th-century marquetry stand, and the sixteen-sided marquetry-topped table.

The set of oak *'occasional' chairs* of slender Gothic design bears the label of 'James Hughes, Upholsterer, Carnarvon, Late of S. J. Waring and Sons Ltd'. The *prie-dieu chair* is stamped by Miles and Edwards, London furniture makers and dealers in fabrics. The *table** with the drawings and lithographs on it is another 'made-up' piece, incorporating 18th-century Dutch inlays and cruder 1830s ones.

The fourteen-day striking *bracket clock* in a Boulle-work case is by Jean le Dieux, Paris, *c.*1700.

Carpet

The carpet is of English manufacture, *c.*1830, from an earlier Savonnerie design.

Metalwork

The tall gilt-bronze *candelabra* at each end of the room are traditionally said to be based on an original by the 16th-century Italian goldsmith Benvenuto Cellini, but there is no precedent for them in his work. They may be the work of a Venetian art foundry of the 1840s.

The two Empire bronze *lamps* on the mantel-piece, in the form of seated classical female figures, with ormolu (gilt bronze) mounts and polished granite bases, have been adapted for electricity. Their original form as oil lamps can be seen in Hawkins's print.

Ceramics

The biscuit porcelain *figures* and *table ornaments* are from parts of two Minton dessert services, *c.*1850, one of them copied from the celebrated 18th-century 'Cameo' service made at Sèvres for Catherine the Great.

Conservation in action

In 1985 the silk lampas (often called brocade) was rewoven especially for the room by Prelle et Cie. of Lyon, copying a fragment of the old fabric found on the massive settee beneath later coverings. At the same time the silk tape for binding the curtains and wall-hangings, the silk rope and gimp for the upholstery, and the glazed woollen 'tammy' lining for the curtains were reproduced in England from original fragments. Since it was not possible to remove the paint to uncover the 2,000 gilt crosses that appear in the lithograph, these had to be reapplied on top of the original ones. At the same time, the carved woodwork was revived and repolished; the unusual pelmets in the form of outsize curtain poles, and the pulleys and rails themselves, were all made by the castle's own craftsmen. The castle carpenter also made a replacement panel for the back of one of the doors, where china shelves had been set up in the early part of the 20th century.

The Ebony Room

Marked as the 'Boudoir' on the earliest plan, the Ebony Room was presumably the morning room where Mrs Dawkins-Pennant and successive Ladies Penrhyn would work at correspondence and household business, and it was here that Alice Douglas-Pennant compiled her catalogue of the pictures, published in 1902.

Here again, different materials are used in disguise, and painted and varnished plaster and polished black limestone in the chimneypiece (from Dinorben near Abergele, or Moelfre on Anglesey) complement the furniture, some of which is in solid ebony, some veneered in ebony, and some of other woods, ebonised to give the same effect.

Furniture

The fashion for ebony furniture had been started by Horace Walpole, and by 1825 it was becoming essential for any house built in an old English style. *Chairs* such as the two low examples (not children's chairs) and the taller single chairs (with legs altered in the 1830s) are probably late 18th-century and may have come from Ceylon, but in Britain they were often supplied by dealers as 'ancient', possibly Tudor. The *armchairs* are of a less exotic style and were probably made in Ceylon in the early 19th century specifically for export. The *settee* may have been made from a design published in Richard Brown's *The Rudiments of Carving Cabinet Furniture and Upholstery* in 1822.

The small *cabinet* with ivory-inlaid ebony veneer is an older piece, possibly 17th-century, from Sindh in India, and the large ebony-veneered *armoire* is Dutch, of the same period. The carved walnut *pole-screens* were supplied to Col. Douglas-Pennant by C. Hindley & Sons around 1845–6.

Picture

92 Studio of Dieric Bouts (d. 1475)
Virgin and Child with St Luke

Legend had it that St Luke painted the Virgin, and hence he is the patron saint of painters. He is shown here making a preliminary drawing in silverpoint, as a contemporary artist would have done. His painted panel stands on an easel in his painting-room on the right of the picture.

The composition is derived from Rogier van der Weyden's treatment of this subject, and ultimately from Jan van Eyck's *Virgin and Child with Chancellor Rolin* in the Louvre. It was bought about 1850 by Edward, Lord Penrhyn and in 1899 was transferred from panel to canvas.

The Ebony Room

Textiles

The magnificent green and crimson fabric (originally on a yellow ground) used for the **curtains**, **upholstery** and **pole-screens** is a silk velvet in a restrained 'bizarre' design, which dates it between 1695 and 1712. Originally these rich velvets were produced in Genoa, although by this date both Lyon and Spitalfields could have woven such a fabric.

The much-faded *c.*1830 Lyon silk brocade used for the **wall-hanging** reproduces part of the same pattern. It was originally ivory, brown and coral red.

The **carpet** is Persian, *c.*1900.

(Right) The richly patterned velvet curtains date from c.1695–1712

The Grand Staircase

The principal staircase must have presented Hopper with a dilemma: how to design a sufficiently impressive stair for such a vast house and yet keep within the Norman style, when he knew that Norman castles had only spiral stone stairs, which could hardly sustain the pitch of the state rooms. He was also very short of space, having only the courtyard of the medieval house (also the site of Samuel Wyatt's 18th-century staircase) to work with. His solution was to make up for this by an orgy of fantastic carving and the use of two contrasting stones: for the walls an oolitic limestone (possibly the Painswick stone of which large blocks were delivered in the late 1820s); and for the carved pylons, balustrades and newels a grey sandstone, possibly from Lancashire. The treads are the same York sandstone used for paving the Grand Hall and corridors.

Lantern

The riot of plaster in the D-shaped panels seems to owe more to the Norse vocabulary of interlace and the Great Beast than to Norman sources. The influence of

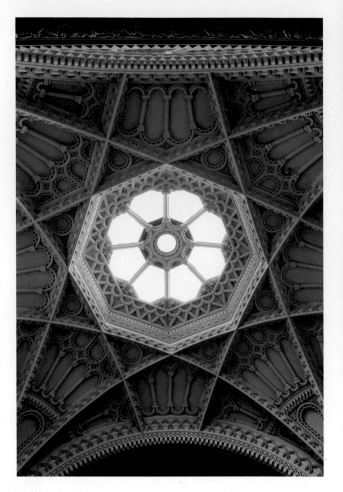

(Above) The plasterwork ceiling of the Grand Staircase

Celtic ornament may also be felt. Above these panels the round skylight with 'column' spokes resembles windows at Helingham and Barfreston churches, near Canterbury, illustrated in Carter's *Ancient Architecture*.

Stained glass

The stained-glass windows are by Thomas Willement and were supplied in 1832.

Lamp brackets

The extraordinary cast-iron lamp brackets, where human arms apparently clasping bows emerge from monstrous mouths, were designed by Hopper.

Carving

Most of the abstract motifs can be found in Carter's *Ancient Architecture*, but many carved components must contain an element of individual invention, such as the corbel-masks at the door jambs and the extraordinary row of human hands around the arch from the Staircase Hall to the Drawing Room.

The newel 'crowns' of the third flight are carved with panels of figures derived from Strutt's *Sports and Pastimes*. The activities depicted are hawking, archery, slinging and elements of the joust and the tournament, and a King of Arms carrying the banners of the two principal barons of the tournament.

(Right) The Grand Staircase

The State Bedroom

This and the adjoining dressing- room are hung with a late 18th-century hand-painted Chinese wallpaper, and share the same bizarre plaster cornice, probably derived from illustrations of Tickencote church by John Carter. The chimneypiece is Penmon limestone.

Furniture

The carved oak *bed*, the *wash-stand* and the *tables de nuit* flanking the bed are Hopper 'Norman' pieces of the 1830s. The bed is hung with silver and blue silk lampas, which is also used for the curtains. The fabric is identical in design, although different in colour, to that used in the Drawing Room. It was rewoven in 1992 by Prelle et Cie to replace the original textiles, which are now too fragile to be shown.

Less obviously of the 1830s is the large carved walnut *armoire*: the figure of Pluto is from Nuremberg, *c.*1530, but his consort Persephone was carved much later, presumably in the 1830s, when the piece was made. The late 17th-century Dutch walnut *cabinet-on-stand* was also altered in the 19th century. The small *circular table* with three spiral-twist legs and stretchers is by C. Hindley & Sons and was probably bought by the 1st Lord Penrhyn.

Some of the other pieces are earlier: the unusual English rococo *looking-glass*, *c.*1725–50, on the window wall is covered with shells and coral fragments, and the *writing-table* below it, with ebony veneer inlaid with floral marquetry, is Louis XIV, *c.*1690.

The painted *mirror* in a giltwood frame over the fireplace is a 19th-century rococo revival piece, inspired by 18th-century Chinese export mirror paintings. On the Louis XIV desk are a mid-19th-century Indian ebony dressing-case and a pair of small 17th-century lacquer cabinets made in Japan.

The State Bedroom

The French eight-day striking *mantel clock* in a gilt brass and porcelain case is signed by Henry Marc, *c.*1880.

Ceramics

On the shelves in the false doorway to the right of the fireplace is part of a Liverpool (impressed Herculaneum) *dessert service* decorated with thistles in the centre. The *wash-stand set* in 'pheasant' pattern is 19th-century Copeland Spode, and the other *bowl and ewer* are from a Minton set decorated in 1894. The Cauldon *china tea set* was supplied by Mortlocks of Oxford Street.

The Grand Hall Gallery

Pictures

The portraits include Sir Joshua Reynolds's *c.*1760 portrait of Richard Pennant*, who transformed the Penrhyn estate (see p. 42). F. R. Lee's *The River Ogwen at Cochwillan Mill*, 1849, was commissioned by the 1st Lord Penrhyn. It shows his great friend General Cartwright watching the artist landing a salmon.

Furniture

The four Ceylonese *ebony chairs* are of the same date (*c.*1800) and design as two in the Ebony Room.

The Passage to the Keep

At ground- and first-floor levels there are passages connecting the principal rooms with the family apartments and bedrooms in the Keep; the two further storeys of the Keep were accessible by spiral staircases in two of the corner turrets, one for service use, and one for the family and guests. Today you can climb the 128 steps from the first floor to the roof, when there is a steward in attendance.

Pictures

The two colourful *West Indian watercolours* are valuable records of the appearance of two of the family's Jamaican plantations – Denbigh and

An English Rococo mirror, c.1725–50, hangs above a Louis XIV writing-desk, c.1690, in the State Bedroom

Pennants – by a local artist in 1871. The sugar factory at Denbigh was built by Richard Pennant in 1802 and was still in use in the 1920s, when new machinery was installed by the 3rd Lord Penrhyn.

Furniture

The four carved oak *side-tables* are from Hopper designs and have Mona Marble and Penmon limestone slab tops. The two Ceylonese *settees* with stamped velvet squabs are early 19th-century in the style of the armchairs in the Ebony Room, but the two single *chairs* are Victorian.

Pictures

The six late 18th-century *watercolours of scenes in Jamaica* are almost certainly connected with the Pennants' Jamaican estates.

The Keep Bedrooms

The suite of rooms shown was probably intended as one apartment, to which the passage hung with watercolours (with its baize door) was the staff access. It would have consisted of a sitting room, a dressing room, bedroom and a small ante-room. The arrangement is followed in the other storeys of the Keep, and it seems likely that one of these apartments was used by the Queen and Prince Consort during their visit on 15 October 1859. The view from the rooms also accords with George Fripp's drawing, made as a record.

For much of the 2nd Lord Penrhyn's time these rooms were used as, respectively, 'Miss Alice Pennant's Room [now shown as a Nursery: her initials are scratched into one of the window panes], Lord Penrhyn's Bedroom, Gertrude Lady Penrhyn's Room, Young Ladies Sitting Room'.

Unlike the principal rooms, the family rooms in the Keep were redecorated in the late 19th century, with wallpapers and fabrics by the firm of Morris & Co. In the first room, probably originally a dressing room, the paper is Morris, 'Double Bough' of 1890, and the hangings of the bed are made from a woven silk and linen fabric called 'Cross Twigs', designed *c.*1894 by J.H. Dearle for Morris & Co.

(Above) The brass bed in the King's Bedroom was used by the Prince of Wales during his visit in 1894

Pictures

William Hayes's *Eleven studies of birds from 'Mr Child's Menagery' at Osterley Park, Middlesex* were commissioned by Robert Child's wife Sarah and published as *Birds in the Collection of Osterley Park* (1779–86), and *Rare and Curious Birds from Osterley Park* (1794).

Furniture

The brass *bed* was ordered, at a cost of £600, for the use of the Prince of Wales when he stayed at Penrhyn in 1894, but it was probably first set up in a room off the Grand Staircase, and originally had different hangings.

The *cheval glass and wash-stand* (with a Mona Marble top) are Hopper designs, as is the hand-knotted Axminster *carpet*, which preserves its original colours better than any of the other 'Norman' examples in the castle.

Ceramics

A pair of Dehan blanc-de-Chine *dogs of Fo*, Kangxi. A 19th-century Chinese *famille rose* trumpet-necked *vase*. A Minton *toilet set* of 'bamboo' design, *c.*1860–70.

The Slate Bed Room

The next bedroom has one of Penrhyn's most famous curiosities. The *slate bed** was probably carved by someone who normally produced slate headstones and chest tombs, a peculiarly Welsh tradition, of which good examples are to be found in Llandygai churchyard. It is hung with a printed cotton called 'Pomegranate', designed by William Morris in 1877.

The *chimneypiece*, one of the most spectacular in the castle, is made of the red Mona Marble; the two *candlesticks* are of the same material, which was also used for the tops of the 'Norman' *night tables*.

Pictures

*Amalfi: birthplace of the mariner's compass** was painted by Clarkson Stanfield, RA (1793–1867), who was one of the most successful early Victorian marine painters. The picture has suffered badly from his use of bitumen to produce rich, transparent darks. It was bought by the 1st Lord Penrhyn in the 1870s.

The *photographs* show members of the 1st and 2nd Barons' families.

Furniture and ceramics

The *seat furniture* is upholstered in what must have been a dazzling green silk fabric of the 1890s. Several

(Right) The bathroom attached to the Slate Bed Room

Hopper-designed pieces include the *dressing-table* and *dressing-mirror*, the massive *wardrobe* with arcaded front, and the *wash-stand*. There are two *wash-stand sets*: the twelve-piece set in blue with gold flower and bird decoration is by Spode, Copeland and Garret, and the part-set in white with pink roses is by Coalport, supplied by T. Goode of London.

The Bathroom

The *wallpaper* is 'Willow Bough', designed by Morris in 1887. The fittings are Shanks's 'Fin de Siècle' models.

The Ante-Room

The Ante-Room adjoining the Bedroom has another Morris *wallpaper*, 'Iris', designed by J. H. Dearle *c.*1887, and a Mona Marble chimneypiece.

Pictures

The watercolours* by George Fennel Robson (1790–1833) were probably painted for George Hay Dawkins-Pennant, since all but one show views of his Caernarfonshire estates.

Furniture

Two Hopper *dressing-tables* and a *table de nuit**. An 1830s carved walnut *armoire* in the 17th-century Swiss style. A Regency rosewood *teapoy** inlaid overall with brass. An American treadle *sewing-machine* by Wheeler and Wilson, 1867. An *armchair* upholstered in William Morris's 'Windrush' block-printed cotton produced in 1883, now much faded.

The Lower India Room

Well into the 19th century the term 'India' was used to denote anything from the Orient. Here it refers to the Chinese hand-painted *wallpaper*, which probably dates from *c.*1800, and would have been set up here in the 1830s. This room was used by the last Lord Penrhyn to live at the castle, Hugh Napier, 4th Baron (1894–1949).

Although their doors have been removed, the positions of the bath and the water-closet in the ante-lobby seem somewhat public. 'The principles of English delicacy are not easily satisfied', wrote Robert Kerr on this subject in his classic *The Gentleman's House* of 1865; '… if the access be too direct, it is a serious error.'

Chimneypiece

The chimneypiece is of mottled Penmon limestone, painted to match the ground colour of the wallpaper.

Furniture

The carved oak *bed, dressing-table, dressing-glass* *, *cheval glass* and *tables de nuit* are all

Hopper designs from the 1830s. Other pieces share the Eastern exoticism of the wallpaper: two Japanese black and gilt *lacquer cabinets**, the one 18th-century on an ebonised stand in the style of William Kent, and the other 17th-century on a much later plain ebonised stand*; a Chinese black and gilt *lacquer tilt-top table*, *c.*1810; and an unusually tall *wardrobe**, assembled *c.*1800 from earlier Chinese panels. The main cupboard doors of this wardrobe are late 17th-century, with figures of horsemen applied in mother-of-pearl and various hardstones; the drawer-fronts are also 17th-century, but the lower doors, decorated with European figures, are 18th-century.

Ceramics

On the mantelpiece are a pair of early 19th-century Chinese *cloisonné vases* and several 18th- and 19th-century Chinese blue-and-white *vessels*. In the corner stands a very large blue-and-white late 19th-century Chinese *vase*. The white and gold china *wash-stand set* is Minton, *c.*1850.

Photograph

On the mantelpiece is a portrait in a slate frame of Sir Prescott Gardner Hewett, Bt (1812–91), a family friend who became Surgeon Extraordinary to Queen Victoria.

The Chapel Corridor

Pictures

Carl Haag's (1820–1915) *Palmyra* and its two companions (Nos. 235 *The Ruins of Baalbec* and 236 *The Acropolis at Athens*)* were commissioned by the 1st Lord Penrhyn after visiting the artist's studio in 1860 with his son George and being 'swept away' by his sketches of the Levant, which the latter knew at first hand. The two ancient cities of Palmyra and Baalbec were rediscovered in 1751 by James Dawkins, uncle of the builder of Penrhyn, and his friend Robert Wood, who together published two influential volumes of engravings of the ruins.

The Chapel

For about 400 years Penrhyn was served by the Chapel whose remains survive in the pleasure ground (set up there as an eye-catcher in the late 18th century). The encaustic *tiles* in the floor of the present chapel are thought to have come from the earlier building, as are the three German 14th-century carved *wooden panels* (probably altar panels) now fitted beneath the stairs from the gallery.

Stained glass

The stained-glass windows are attributed to David Evans of Shrewsbury. In the gallery window, which closely resembles Evans's work at St Giles, Shrewsbury, there are two scenes: in the upper part, the *Adoration of the Magi*, and in the lower the *Nunc dimittis* episode, loosely copied from the right-hand panel of Rubens's *Descent from the Cross* triptych at Antwerp.

The Secondary Staircase

It was built immediately next to the Grand Stairs, so that staff and members of the family or guests should not meet on the same stair.

The Grand Hall (Aisles)

Stained glass

At close quarters, Willement's ingenuity in suggesting antiquity in the round panels of his great windows can be appreciated more clearly. He used fragments of actual medieval glass (in the blue colours, for example), and 'distressed' other areas by flicking specks of paint on to the surface to suggest the

pitting caused by corrosion on the outside of old windows. [*Please do not touch the glass*]

Furniture

Beneath the windows are two massive stone *tables*, both designed by Hopper. The first is of slate, probably enamelled by G. E. Magnus to resemble black marble, with a zig-zag motif painted on the top slab to simulate inlaid granite. The other table is of the mottled Penmon lime-stone seen elsewhere in the castle.

(Right) The Chapel in 1846; lithograph by G. Hawkins

(Above) The Chapel

Pictures

Henry Tanworth Wells's portrait of *Edward Gordon Douglas-Pennant, 1st Lord Penrhyn of Llandegai* (1800–86) was painted in 1869. Lord Penrhyn's youngest daughter Adela records: 'The sittings were very tedious to my Father, in spite of his appreciation of the good will which had caused their infliction, and when my Mother could not accompany him he used often to take me with him, although I was only a child, to Mr Wells' studio to help to while away the time.' Presented by subscription to the Town Hall, Caernarfon, and subsequently given to the National Trust.

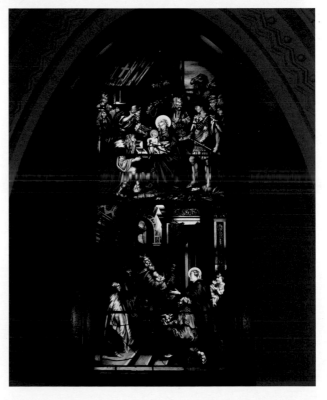

(Right) The Adoration of the Magi; stained-glass window attributed to David Evans of Shrewsbury

The Dining Room

Decoration

In the ceiling, the standard repertoire of Norman motifs may have been enriched by the study of West Indian botanical forms. The 20 principal leaf-bosses are encircled by bands of figurative mouldings derived from the south arch of the Norman church of Kilpeck, Herefordshire. The smaller bosses in rows dividing the larger compartments were originally much more numerous.

The use of stencilled decoration on walls and ceilings is not unusual at this date, but its extent here, covering the entire wall area above the dado, is apparently without parallel. It was an ingenious way of providing 'Norman' decoration on a flat surface. In the early 20th century the stencilling was painted over, and only revealed once again in 1974.

The massive statuary *chimneypiece* is carved from highly polished black Penmon limestone. The supporting figures are loosely derived from the famous antique Roman figures now in the Museo Nazionale at Naples and known as the 'Farnese captives' or 'Captive barbarians', a rare classical source for the decoration at Penrhyn.

Pictures

On the fireplace wall hang full-length portraits of Richard Pennant and his wife Anne Warburton (who was joint-heiress to the Penrhyn estate and is dressed in Turkish costume), and of Edward Gordon Douglas-Pennant, 1st Lord Penrhyn of Llandegai (who inherited Penrhyn through his first wife, Juliana). The end wall is filled by Richard Brompton's huge 1773 portrait of Henry Dawkins and his family. The small boy with his hand on the greyhound is Dawkins's son George, who built Penrhyn.

The Dining Room

Furniture

Three of the carved *buffets* (or side-tables) are made of burr or pollard oak, and the five dining-tables are veneered in the same material. The fourth sideboard table is of carved oak and, though contemporary with the castle, it is not a Hopper design. Around the table are 20 *ebony chairs* with stamped velvet seats, all of the 1830s, and some of the earlier species of ebony and ebonised chairs are set around the walls.

The mid-18th-century French eight-day striking *clock* in a Boulle-work case was given a new movement by Welch of Bangor in the 19th century.

Textiles

The carpet (an English 'Savonnerie') dates from the early 1830s. The plush curtains, introduced in 1997, are similar to those which would have hung here originally. The stamped pattern, called 'Fronsac', was made in France by Claremont. Similar examples from the 1840s can be seen on the dining-chairs.

Sculpture and ornament

On the mantelpiece stand two pairs of 19th-century *tazze* (shallow bowls on feet) carved in a very fine-grained polished black limestone, possibly from Ireland or mainland Europe; and a pair of polished black limestone candlesticks designed by Hopper. On the buffets flanking the chimneypiece is a pair of 18th-century Swedish porphyry *urns*. On the sideboard at the south end of the room are a pair of Siena marble *tazze* with bronze 'dolphin' stands, c.1830, and a Penmon marble obelisk. On the buffet at the north end is a *granite figure of Osiris*, Egyptian, XXVI Dynasty (650 BC), possibly acquired by the 2nd Lord Penrhyn.

Metalwork

The silver includes a pair of George III *tureens* *and covers* * by Thomas Robins, 1809, and a set of Regency salt cellars by Paul Storr, 1816. The *flatware* on the dining-table, bearing the arms of Richard Pennant, 1st Lord Penrhyn, is all by Thomas Heming, 1771–80. The *racing trophies* down the centre were all won by the 2nd and

A chamber for chamberpots

It was a very long way from here to the 'necessary offices', and at one end of the dado on the window wall a 'secret' cupboard was fitted to accommodate Burleighware chamberpots, presumably for use only after the ladies and staff had withdrawn.

3rd Barons' racehorses: The Clifden Cup*, 1869, takes the form of a partly gilt group of Elizabeth I on a royal progress, with a relief of Burghley House on the plinth, by Elkington & Co. It was won by 'Vagabond'. The Newmarket July Cup*, 1890, a George III silver-gilt vase, 1808, was won by 'Queen of the Fairies'.

The Queen's Gold Vase*, Ascot, 1894, a silver-gilt wine cistern bearing the Royal Arms and with a relief of charioteers on one side, by Garrards, was won by 'Quaesitum'.

The Goodwood Cup*, 1898, a William IV silver-gilt vase by Emes & Barnard, 1825, was won by 'King's Messenger'.

Also on the dining-table are a pair of Louis XV-style ormolu seven-branch *candelabra* and two from a set of large early 19th-century ormolu *oil lamps* with stands in the form of altar candlesticks.

The Breakfast Room

When only the family was in residence and the full complement of footmen in black and gold striped waistcoats, tail-coats and gloves was not required in the large Dining Room, meals would be taken here.

Chimneypiece

The presence of a single bearded male head in the centre of the mantelpiece, carved in the mottled grey Penmon limestone, is a mystery. There are many other hirsute heads in plaster and stone around the castle, and these may all allude to the medieval wild men or 'wodehouses', as the antiquarian Joseph Strutt called them.

Pictures

The cream of Penrhyn's fine collection of Old Masters is displayed here. It is a rare survival in Britain of a 19th-century collection and was largely assembled by Edward Gordon Douglas-Pennant, 1st Baron Penrhyn, with the advice of the Belgian dealer C.J. Nieuwenhuys. It includes Holy Families by Palma Vecchio* and Perino del Vaga, landscapes by Bellotto*, Canaletto* and Guardi*, Spanish portraits and – last, but not least – Rembrandt's *Portrait of Catrina Hoogsaet* of 1657.

Furniture and ornaments

The oak *buffet-table* on the right-hand wall is another of Hopper's designs with a polished Penmon limestone top. The other, mahogany, *sideboard table* is similar to the one in the Dining Room, and not by Hopper. The small oak William IV *dining-table* is inlaid with burr walnut. It has two further leaves. Around the

The Breakfast Room

walls are several more of the ebony chairs seen elsewhere in the castle. The impressive *armchairs** with lion masks on the arms and stuffed backs either side of the chimneypiece are partly ebonised, partly ebony-veneered, and incorporate earlier (George II) legs. They were probably made up by Hopper.

The two small two-handled *vases* on the mantelpiece are of the same fine-grained black limestone as the *tazze* in the Dining Room, and are decorated with Egyptian hieroglyphs, possibly by the Derby Marble Works, *c.*1850. The font-shaped black marble *bowl* may have been designed by Hopper. The *pole-screen banner* is embroidered with the arms of Edward Gordon Douglas-Pennant, 1st Baron Penrhyn of Llandegai, and his second wife Lady Maria Louisa Fitzroy.

The fourteen-day French bracket *clock* in a Boulle-work case is by Daniel Boucheret, Paris, *c.*1710.

Metalwork

The two Regency bronze *Argand lamps** have been converted to electricity. The base of the ormolu *candelabrum* on the table is probably an Italian altar candlestick, with later arms added. The pair of two-handled bronze *urns* after the Antique on the mantelpiece is 19th-century. Their design combines the form of the Medici Vase with the decoration of the equally famous Borghese Vase.

Ceramics

The large *punchbowl* on the 'Norman' table by the window is Chinese in the Imari style, 18th-century.

The Passage from the Breakfast Room

Pictures

Henry Hawkins's *The Penrhyn Slate Quarry* (dated 1832) was probably painted for George Dawkins-Pennant in the year of Princess Victoria's visit to the quarry. The Princess wrote in her journal on 8 September 1832: 'It was very curious to see the men split the slate, and others cut it while others hung suspended by ropes and cut the slate; others again drove wedges into a piece of rock and in that manner would split off a block. Then little carts about a dozen at a time rolled down a railway by themselves…' The picture depicts the quarry from the lower side, showing in the middle distance Talcen Mawr or 'Gibraltar rock', blown up in 1895, and evidently contains a number of portraits.

The portrait probably depicts Lady Juliana Dawkins (1726–70), who was the mother of George Hay Dawkins-Pennant.

Catrina Hooghsaet, by Rembrandt, is the masterpiece of the collection. It was bought by the 1st Lord Penrhyn about 1860

The Staff Quarters

Beyond the Breakfast Room the principal rooms of the castle were divided from the domain of the servants by two oak doors, each four inches thick; these, and the sharp bend in the corridor, would prevent the migration of sounds and kitchen smells from one side to the other.

The Servants' Hall

The junior staff would assemble here three times a day for meals. Since it overlooks the entrance forecourt, the windows are set high enough to prevent observation, inward or out. Located near the back door, it also served as the waiting room for tradesmen. The cast-iron cooking range is a combined open and close fire double oven.

The Housekeeper's Room

Beyond the door in the passage, this was the principal office of the household. It is now the tea-room.

Each morning, Lady Penrhyn would meet the housekeeper here, and they would decide the daily duties. The housekeeper, butler and lady's maid had their meals together here and it was also the setting for discipline and dismissals.

The Lamp Room

The Still Room

Cakes, jams, tea and coffee were prepared here, and it served as the main kitchen when the family was away.

The Housekeeper's Store

Linen and cleaning materials were kept here in what is now the tea-room annexe.

> ### Contents of the Housekeeper's Store in 1833
>
> '14 lbs Best Yellow Soap, 14 lbs Mottled Soap, 1 lb Rotten stone (a polishing powder), 1 lb putty powder [a powder of calcinated tin, for polishing glass or metal], 6 yds scouring flannel, 3 lbs Pot Ash, 3 lbs Soda, 3 wash leathers, 1 Plate Brush, 2 lbs Poland Starch, ½ lb Thumb Blue [washing indigo in small lumps], 2 lbs Rush Candles, 10 lbs Dip Candles, 2 Blk. Lead Brushes, etc. etc.'.

The Servants' Bedrooms

The Housemaids' Tower provided the sleeping accommodation, in separate bedrooms, for the junior female staff. Strict segregation was maintained between this tower and the Footmen's Tower, at the corner of the stable block, where the junior male servants slept.

The Fuel Stores and Brushing Room

Down the stairs, between the domestic and kitchen offices, were, on the left, the Coal Vault (132 tons were consumed in 1830), and the Brushing Room, furnished simply with one large table for the brushing of clothes.

The Oil Vault and Lamp Room

On the other side of the passage are the Oil Vault and the Lamp Room where, through the window, you can see how the oil lamps were cleaned, filled and trimmed. Electric lighting was only introduced by the 4th Lord Penrhyn, and as late as 1900 194 lamps had to be trimmed and lit every day during winter.

The Cook's Sitting Room

The China Room

All the tableware used by the family was stored here under the supervision of the Housekeeper. Entertainment on a scale enjoyed by 1st Lord and Lady Penrhyn required a vast store of dessert and dinner service. Just one of the Minton dinner services stored here included 114 dinner plates, and there was also a magnificent Minton dessert service.

The Cook's Sitting Room

Back along the corridor to the right is the Cook's Sitting Room. The Cook was perhaps the most important member of staff, given the ambitious catering laid on for visitors to Penrhyn, and as a result was given the highest level of comfort and a £150 per year salary.

The servant community at Penrhyn

A strict hierarchy operated, with the housekeeper at the head, and the butler, 1st lady's maid, 1st footman and 1st housemaid following in order of precedence. Joining the household at sixteen, an undermaid (there were seven housemaids in 1883) would spend almost her entire time cleaning the staff rooms, gradually learning the work of the different departments, for instance by laying the table for the housekeeper's meals. Similarly, a young footman spent time waiting on the housekeeper and other senior staff before he could take on the same duties in the Dining Room.

In 1883, at the height of the Victorian period, the establishment consisted of 23 female housemaids, kitchen and laundry staff, and eleven male household staff, with seven in the stables.

The Pastry Pantry

Through the door of the Pastry Pantry can be seen plates of rich desserts laid out as if waiting to be served to the Prince and Princess of Wales and other guests. These are displayed on pieces from the 1850s Minton dessert service.

The Kitchen

This vast kitchen is shown as it looked during preparations for one of the banquets, and a few of the menus are framed and hang on the far wall. The great roasting range was operated by a rack-and-pinion mechanism mounted within each hob. In front a large roasting screen protected the kitchen staff from the intense heat of the fire. Once cooked, the dishes were placed in the adjacent hot-cupboard ready for sending up to the Dining Room.

The Pastry Room

The long slate benches lining two of its walls were ideal for pastry-making, and the square slate pastry board and slate rolling pin were made by a quarryman at Lord Penrhyn's Bethesda quarries. The flour was stored in the lidded bin and the mixing bowls are marked 'K' for kitchen.

The royal visit in 1894

Between 10 and 13 July 1894 Penrhyn Castle experienced some of its grandest entertaining in honour of the visit of the Prince and Princess of Wales (later King Edward VII and Queen Alexandra). There was a nine-course dinner in the evening followed by an evening party for over 200 guests, which was rounded off with a supper at midnight featuring truffled quail, lobster, foie gras and every other available delicacy. Over the course of three days the kitchens had prepared over 1,150 individual meals, including 89 separate dishes of the greatest gastronomic quality, served to each of the 35 house-guests.

The Scullery

This was where foods were prepared prior to cooking and where the utensils were washed. In the corner are the boilers, one of which was for boiling large joints of meat and for producing hot water for washing and cleaning purposes. Alongside this, the wall is lined with shelves and lockers for vegetables and above is the bacon-loft.

The Larders

To the north of the scullery are the larders: the Wet Larder for uncooked meats, the Dry Larder for cooked food, and the Dairy Larder, which is shown as if being used for making ice-cream and for moulding butter. The hygienic benefits of storing uncooked foods completely separately from cooked ones were well understood at Penrhyn.

Return to the passage and go out into the kitchen courtyard.

(Left) The Pastry Pantry   *(Right) The Kitchen*

The Garden and Pleasure Ground

The grounds of the castle which the visitor sees today are typical Georgian pleasure grounds, embellished with later Victorian planting and set in extensive designed parkland (not the property of the National Trust), which makes full use of the magnificent 'borrowed landscape' of Snowdonia, the Menai Strait and Great Orme's Head.

The 'bones' of the present landscape seem to date from the late 18th century and the house designed by Samuel Wyatt. There was much planting in the early 19th century at the time the present castle was being built, including many newly introduced exotic species, which, by late Victorian times, were celebrated as among the finest specimens of their species in the British Isles. However, Penrhyn's greatest horticultural glory was achieved under the head gardenership of Walter Speed from c.1860 to 1921, when the estate was famed for the unsurpassed quality of its kitchen garden produce.

The lost medieval garden

The earliest surviving plan of the grounds, surveyed by G. Leigh in 1768, shows the medieval house set in a landscape of small enclosures, many of them planted with trees.

Eucryphias in flower

The approach to the house is shown striking off at right angles to the drive across an outer court-yard, through the stable block and up to the front door of the house. South of the house is an area quartered by paths, which was probably a formal garden. The rectangular area immediately north of the house, convenient for the stables and a plentiful supply of manure, is likely to have been a kitchen garden. Several other areas are described as *gardd* or garden, notably the site of the present walled garden (Gardd Parc y Moch or Pig Park Garden) and Gardd Bryn Dillad (Clothes Hill Garden, perhaps a drying green), at the foot of the slope below the castle, roughly at the point along the drive from which the visitor now sees the first view of the Keep. Three orchard enclosures are shown on the east-facing slopes below the house.

The late 18th-century garden

The plan of 1804 by Robert Williams, a reputable land surveyor living in Bangor, shows the landscape remodelled in the English style. The new Wyatt house is shown with the stable block moved to the north. We do not know who was responsible for this new landscape design, but it is clear that the grounds have been remodelled at very considerable expense. Pleasure grounds have been created around the house and the old medieval chapel moved to the north-west of the house as an eye-catcher, appropriate in style to the new Gothic house. An interesting system of paths or drives has been created south-east of the house, extensive belts and some clumps have been planted and other areas cleared of trees to open up vistas.

The landscaping of the grounds seems to have started as early as 1780. The skilful composition of this new landscape suggests the involvement of an experienced landscaper: William Emes (1730–1803) or his foreman, and later partner, John Webb (1754–1828) have been suggested, but there remains no proof. Both worked in Wales, and Emes created the landscapes for several houses built or remodelled by Samuel Wyatt, the closest being Baron Hill on Anglesey (1776–9).

The castle garden

The building of the castle by George Hay Dawkins-Pennant seems to have been accompanied by an energetic new phase of planting and landscaping. A letter survives from Messrs Austin & McAslan, Nursery & Seedsmen, Glasgow, to Dawkins-Pennant hoping for his further patronage:

We hope the trees sent you in 1822 & '23 are giving satisfaction, therefore we take the liberty of sending you a list of our prices for the season which we hope you will consider very reasonable; the Oaks, Sycamores and Ash are remarkably fine but indeed they are all in general very good; if you think of planting this season, your planting orders will have the shortest attention. We are sincerely obliged for recommending us to Viscount Kirkwall who has got a large quantity from us.

Exotic introductions

Few records remain of the further planting of the grounds by Dawkins-Pennant and his successor, Edward Gordon Douglas-Pennant, but it is clear that both must have been enthusiastic planters, adding many exotic and newly introduced species to the basic framework of native species which had been established by the 1820s. The tithe map of 1841 shows the landscape near the castle little changed in outline from the map of 1804; however, a very large area north of the castle, shown as fields in 1804, has been turned into parkland generously planted with belts and clumps of trees. This new planting was clearly designed to enhance the carriage drives through this area and to provide splendid views across the Menai Strait and eastwards to Great Orme's Head.

The new castle required changes to the landscape made for the earlier house, not least the creation of a new drive to approach the castle from the east instead of the west. The old drive was kept for some years after the building of the castle and appears in some illustrations of the then new house. To the south of the new drive it is still possible to detect the landscaping of the woodland with glades and vistas, plus a liberal scattering of the then newly introduced trees and shrubs sent back from America and China by intrepid plant hunters such as David Douglas, Robert Fortune and the brothers Lobb from the 1820s to the 1850s. Most of the exotic trees planted at this time have succumbed to old age and the fierce gales of recent years, but many were recorded in the 1880s by Angus Duncan Webster, then Head Forester. Their sizes suggest that most were planted in the late 1830s or shortly after the succession of Edward Gordon Douglas-Pennant in 1840. Although Douglas the plant hunter was not related, it is easy to imagine that Douglas-Pennant relished growing his namesake's firs: two recorded by Webster were among the oldest and finest in the country, probably planted between 1836 and 1841; the two which remain on either side of the lodge do not appear in the lithograph of 1846, but were probably planted by Douglas-Pennant shortly thereafter.

By the time of the visit of Queen Victoria in 1859, the landscape must have been approaching maturity, all the planting enhancing the magnificent views as the landscapers had intended. Victoria recorded in her diary for 17 October:

After breakfast I went out with Col. & Ly. Pennant, our children & almost all the company & planted 2 trees in Albert's & my name. Arthur [her son, the Duke of Connaught] also planted one. The day cleared & became fine & I walked with our hosts & the 3 girls in the very fine grounds. The view on the sea with Pen Man Mear [Penmaemawr] rising above it, is very beautiful.

The Queen's tree, a Wellingtonia (*Sequoiadendron giganteum*, introduced from California by William Lobb in 1835) was the first of many

---

Second to none

'As a gardener nothing that Mr Speed did but he did well. As a Grape grower he was certainly second to none. Who that had seen his old faggot of Vines, pruned in his own inimitable way, will ever forget the monster bunches he grew each year, and their perfect finish? Most of his Peaches under glass he lifted and replanted each year and fed with new loam. I have seen them grown as well, but never better. His Fig trees on walls out of doors, to see them in fruit was a sight never to be forgotten. Carnations and plants generally under glass were well done. The old-fashioned walled in flower garden near to the castle was a veritable gem when in full beauty in late summer.'

The Garden magazine on Walter Speed, 1921

(Above) The Walled Garden in late summer

ceremonial plantings on the Chapel Lawn west of the castle and is one of only two remaining. Edward VII, when Prince of Wales, and his sisters Princess Maud and Princess Victoria planted trees on a visit in 1894; others were planted by the Queen of Romania, Stanley Baldwin and Anthony Eden in 1890, 1932 and 1937 respectively.

Two great gardeners

Starting his employment at Penrhyn a few years after the Queen's visit, Walter Speed reigned as Head Gardener here for 58 years under three Lords Penrhyn. He was renowned as a leading expert on the production of fruit and flowers and as a strict yet kind-hearted disciplinarian who turned Penrhyn into a centre of horticultural excellence famed throughout Britain. Speed was one of the original recipients of horticulture's highest award, the Victoria Medal

of Honour, in 1897. Penrhyn's horticultural glory continued under Speed's son-in-law and successor, Mr Kneller.

Angus Duncan Webster, a Scot like the 1st Lord Penrhyn, was another particularly eminent employee of the Penrhyn estate, working as Head Forester from about 1880 until the early 1890s. His interests were not confined to trees and his many publications included several written at Penrhyn, such as *British Orchids* (1886) and *Forest Flora of Carnarvonshire, More Particularly the Penrhyn Estate* (1885). His records of trees at Penrhyn give a valuable insight into the planting of the estate. Webster went on to become Chief Forester to the Duke of Bedford at Woburn Abbey in 1893 where he was remembered as the last of the 'top-hatted, tail-coated foresters' who rode round the woods in the mornings and were driven round in a gig in the afternoons. He became Superintendent of Regent's Park in 1896, a post which he held until 1920, when he emigrated to the United States.

Memories of Penrhyn

Hubert George Scrivener came to Penrhyn as an apprentice when he was in his late teens in 1906. His diary for 1908 starts assiduously in January but peters out by the summer, when evening work or other distractions seem to have taken priority. The daily tasks of an apprentice gardener are set out along with lists of bedding and other plants. Even such a sketchy record shows clearly the accumulated expertise of the kitchen gardener and the precise attention to strict regimes that was essential to achieve satisfactory results.

The quantity and variety of produce are impressive: almost 3,000 bedding geraniums; early sweet peas in pots and late ones planted outside in twenty varieties; some 400 indoor chrysanthemums and others outside; large quantities of begonias, stocks and China Asters. There is also a list of exactly the same sort of slightly tender shrubs and climbers that we find in the walled garden today.

But it is the memoirs of John Elias Jones and Arthur F. Brown, both at Penrhyn during the 1920s, that most vividly paint a picture of the workings of the kitchen garden and its social strata. The 'inside staff' consisted of between six and eight journeymen gardeners, one 'garden boy', and the foreman, all of whom lived in the bothy, a fairly large house adjoining the kitchen garden. Most of the journeymen slept in a large

> ### Tasks for January 1908
> Washing nectarine trees; putting 60 pots of beans in; starting hotbed for cucumbers; boxing geraniums; potting gladioli; starting early peach house; putting strawberries in early peach house; inserting chrysanthemum cuttings; sowing 381 pots of sweet peas; starting fig house.

room separated by partitions, each cubicle having its own single bed, wardrobe, chest of drawers and chair. The total garden staff could rise to as many as 30 in the summer, and the Head Gardener was responsible for some 50 estate staff in all.

Lord and Lady Penrhyn were only usually in residence during August for grouse shooting and from October to Christmas for pheasant shooting, but during their absence produce from the kitchen garden was sent to them, each fruit individually wrapped and bunches of grapes packed so that they arrived in pristine condition, their bloom intact.

The gardeners' day began at 7am and finished at 6pm in winter with a half-hour break for breakfast and an hour for lunch. Summer hours were longer, and journeymen had also to work on Saturday and Sunday mornings. Mr Jones recalls a starting wage of 8s per week (presumably after deductions for board), Mr Brown remembering the princely sum of 22s, which even after deductions allowed the occasional Saturday night out and a flutter on the horses.

Since the 1920s

It was during Jones's and Brown's time at Penrhyn in the late 1920s that Sybil, Lady Penrhyn altered and developed the walled flower garden. Although the walls appear to date from the building of the Wyatt house, the garden was and remains predominantly Victorian in character. Lady Penrhyn altered the beds on the terrace, replaced the conservatory there with the existing loggia, and created a water garden in the area below the lower walk.

> ### A wonderful training
> 'Everybody had the opportunity to go through all the different departments, and although one is never finished learning in gardening, we had a methodical, strict and wonderful training, and in 5 years it would be your own fault if you were not fit to go and take on more responsibility in any other good garden. There are many men in different parts of the country today who are very grateful for the training they received at Penrhyn.'
>
> John Elias Jones

The fuchsia walk, praised in a *Country Life* article of 1903 as 'the real glory of Penrhyn' which 'would be the wonder of a county in England', ran down the path from the centre of the terrace. Although there are reports of fuchsias here during the last war, when much of the garden was turned over to growing vegetables, the walk must by then have become suppressed by the magnificent eucryphias on either side. The walk has been reinstated along the south-west side of the garden using *Fuchsia* 'Riccartonii' and the original ironwork.

In the 1930s and 1940s Hugh Napier, 4th Lord Penrhyn, established a rhododendron walk to the north-west of the castle, which includes a very large group of *Rhododendron yunnanense* and a particularly fine form of *R. decorum*, which seems to be unique to Penrhyn. Since Penrhyn became the property of the National Trust in 1951, the garden has been maintained with a fraction of the original staff while keeping most of its original character. Severe gales have depleted the stock of exotic specimen trees, all too liable to wind-blow on the shallow soil overlying rock. However, a vigorous policy of replanting, and careful management of resources have ensured that Penrhyn can retain its 19th-century splendour for generations to come.

(Right) The Fuchsia Arch in the Walled Garden

The early owners of Penrhyn

The society of 13th-century North Wales had changed little for centuries. It was a world of rural communities of free and bondmen with few large settlements, subject to the personal rule of the local Welsh prince and liable to be disrupted by periodic invasion from England. During the 13th century, land settlement and ownership gradually became more defined, and the prizes for those who successfully acquired land could be vast.

Men in the political service of the Princes of Gwynedd at that time could expect to be rewarded with large tracts of land, free from any due or service. The most notable examples of such rewarding must be the cases of Ednyfed Fychan (d. 1246), seneschal (or steward) to the prince, Llywelyn ab Iorwerth, and his sons Goronwy ab Ednyfed (d. 1268) and Tudur ab Ednyfed (d. 1278). These three men were rewarded with large areas of land in many parts of North Wales and as far south as Dyfed.

Part of the lands given to Goronwy ab Ednyfed was a promontory containing over 500 acres of land, immediately east of Bangor, which has been known for centuries as Penrhyn (literally meaning 'promontory'). The holding passed to Goronwy's descendants and their families, who grew independent of each other until the late 14th century.

Gwilym ap Gruffydd: Founder of the estate

In the late 14th century Gwilym ap Gruffydd married Morfudd, daughter of Goronwy Fychan of Penmynydd, Anglesey, who held the other share of Penrhyn. Thus Gwilym was able to reunite Penrhyn, which became the centre of the estate he was to build – the first large landed estate in North Wales.

Political events, however, were to intervene. In September 1400 Owain Glyndŵr was proclaimed Prince of Wales and entered into open rebellion against the English crown. The uncles of Gwilym ap Gruffydd's wife, Morfudd,

'If one dared … to compare the Court of God on high … with an earthly court. The appearance of Gwilym's court … is more like … the cloister of God than the court of man'.

15th-century Welsh poet Rhys Goch Eryri

were close relatives of Owain Glyndŵr and were amongst his staunchest supporters. Gwilym himself held aloof for some time, but joined the rebellion in 1402. In 1406 he surrendered to the English king, Henry IV, and the following year his lands became forfeit to the crown because of his part in the rebellion. Yet within eight months he had succeeded in buying back his own lands. Later he was also able to purchase those of his relatives forfeited during the rebellion. During this period Morfudd died, and Gwilym then married Joan Stanley, daughter of Sir William Stanley of Hooton, Cheshire. This was a crucial marriage, which established a close connection that was to last for over a century with the Stanley family, who were already powerful landowners in the North West.

From about 1410 Gwilym's estate began to grow rapidly. At some time between 1410 and his death in 1431 he built a fortified manor house with its own tower and chapel at Penrhyn, which stood more or less intact until about 1786.

William Griffith I, II and III

Gwilym died in 1431, the founder of an estate based on inheritance, marriage, purchase, enterprise and political wisdom. He was succeeded at Penrhyn by his son from his second marriage, who became known as William Griffith or Gwilym Fychan. In 1443 William Griffith I was released from the restrictions of

(Right) The west front of medieval Penrhyn

the penal laws that Henry IV had imposed on Welshmen following the suppression of Owain Glyndŵr's rebellion, on the condition that he married an Englishwoman and held no public office. In 1447 he married Alice Dalton of Apethorpe, Northamptonshire, who had Stanley family connections. Throughout William's life the Penrhyn estate continued to grow, mostly now by purchase. Like his father, he bought lands in Bangor, Llandygai and Anglesey and towards the end of his life turned his attention to the Llŷn Peninsula.

He was succeeded in 1483 by his son, also called William Griffith. The latter was appointed Chamberlain of North Wales by Richard III in 1483 and married Joan Troutbeck, a niece of Sir Thomas Stanley, later to become the 1st Earl of Derby. Just before the defeat and death of Richard III at Bosworth in 1485, William Griffith was dragged into the vortex of a political storm, probably because of his connections with the Stanley family. It had become obvious to Richard that Sir Thomas Stanley held the military balance in England, and in order to secure his allegiance he imprisoned his son, George Stanley, Lord Strange, in Nottingham Castle, together with William Griffith, his kinsman. Both men survived, and their families flourished under the new king, the Welshman

Henry VII. William Griffith was made a Knight Bachelor in 1489 and remained Chamberlain until his death in 1505–6.

Sir William Griffith was succeeded by his son, also called William Griffith. The third William Griffith was an Esquire of the Body of the King in 1509 and was appointed Chamberlain of North Wales in the same year. One of his fellow esquires was Charles Brandon, later to become Duke of Suffolk. William Griffith subsequently served under Brandon during the English expedition against France in 1513, and was knighted in the field at Tournai.

On the second Sir William's death in 1531 the Penrhyn estate passed to his son, Edward, a professional soldier who saw service in Ireland. In 1540 Edward died of dysentery in Dublin Castle, leaving a wife, Jane Puleston, three young daughters, Jane, Catherine and Ellen, and a brother, Rhys Griffith. Following his death, disputes arose as to his true heirs which led to court action. After two years the court made an award which, in effect, was to split up the medieval Penrhyn estate. Most of the Anglesey lands were to be divided between Edward Griffith's three daughters, while the Caernarfonshire lands, including Penrhyn, were to go to Rhys Griffith. Decades of litigation followed.

Pyrs Griffith: 'A notable pirate'

Rhys Griffith, who was knighted in 1547, died in 1580, and was succeeded by the eldest son of his third marriage, Pyrs Griffith, then aged twelve. Pyrs Griffith is perhaps the most enigmatic and interesting member of the Griffith family. There are many legends concerning him. He is said to have been a pirate or a privateer; to have taken part in the campaign against the Armada in 1588 and to have had a secret tunnel built from Abercegin (later Port Penrhyn) to Penrhyn Castle. There is a certain amount of documentary evidence to support the legends. He was a poet, and all his surviving Welsh poems concern the sea. He did capture a Spanish ship, the *Speranza of Ayamonte*, in 1600 and brought it to Abercegin with a cargo of olive oil, earthernware and silk. In 1603 he was arrested on board his ship in Cork harbour by a Captain Charles Plessington, who described him as 'Captain Pierce Griffith, a notable pirate'.

Pyrs Griffith had come into his inheritance in 1591, but continued to spend much time at sea. A fellow poet, seafarer and landowner, Thomas Prys of Plas Iolyn (?1564–1634), wrote several poems to Pyrs Griffith. In one he sends a porpoise from the Menai Strait to Spanish waters to bring Pyrs Griffith back to his home and his lands:

May God of his grace give him as a treasure
Grace to depart from the sea.

In 1616 his father-in-law, Sir Thomas Mostyn, had Pyrs Griffith put in the Fleet prison in London for non-payment of monies due under his marriage settlement. In the following year the Penrhyn estate passed to Ievan Lloyd of Iâl, to whom large parts of it had already been mortgaged. Thus the connection between the Griffith family and Penrhyn came to an end. Pyrs died in 1628 and was buried in Westminster Abbey.

The Williams family

In 1622 Ievan Lloyd sold the Penrhyn estate to John Williams, a descendant of Robin ap Gruffydd, Gwilym ap Gruffydd's brother, and thus a distant kinsman of Pyrs Griffith. John Williams's purchase reunited Penrhyn with the neighbouring Cochwillan estate, for the hall-house at Cochwillan had been built by Gwilym ap Gruffydd's great-nephew and namesake between 1452 and 1480.

John Williams (1582–1650) was successively Dean of Salisbury and of Westminster, Lord Keeper of the Great Seal, Bishop of Lincoln and Archbishop of York. Thomas Pennant, the celebrated naturalist and topographer, and distant relative of the Pennants of Penrhyn, gives a full and unflattering account of his life, considering him '… as a wise but not as a good man … a great minister but a bad divine'. When a child at Conwy he would play at leaping from the medieval town walls to the shore; and on one occasion 'the fall was on so critical a part,' wrote Pennant, 'as ever to secure him from all reproaches of unchastity'. At the start of the Civil War in 1642 he was entrusted by the King with the defence of Conwy. Ousted from the command of Conwy in 1645, he promptly offered his services to the Parliamentarian Sir John Mytton in laying siege to the castle. The news of the King's execution affected him deeply and he died at Gloddaeth, near Conwy, in 1650. His kneeling effigy in Llandygai church is accompanied by a helm and spurs. On his death the Penrhyn estate (as the two estates will be referred to henceforth) passed to his

nephew, Griffith Williams. Emulating his uncle, Griffith Williams served at different times the Commonwealth, the Protectorate and (after 1660) the King. In 1658 he became one of the thirteen baronets created by Cromwell. The honour was annulled at the Restoration, but recreated by Charles II in 1661.

Griffith Williams died in 1663 and was succeeded by his eldest son, Sir Robert Williams, 2nd Baronet, who married a daughter of Sir John Glynne, an ambitious lawyer of Hawarden in Flintshire. Glynne imposed such a severe marriage settlement on his son-in-law that the couple were forced to leave Penrhyn and live in Chester. In 1680 Sir Robert was succeeded by his elder son, Sir John Williams, 3rd Baronet, who died without issue two years later. His brother, Sir Griffith, 4th Baronet, fared no better and died in 1684. At this point the title and estate went separate ways, the title passing to Sir Robert Williams's brother, Hugh.

The estate remained effectively intact throughout the first half of the 18th century, but ownership became increasingly fragmented among the 2nd Baronet's descendants. In 1767 Anne, Lady Yonge, sold her portion to John and Henry Pennant, sons of Edward Pennant of Clarendon, Jamaica.

(Left)
John Williams, Archbishop of York (1582–1650), who acquired the Penrhyn estate in 1622

(Right)
Sir Griffith Williams, 1st Baronet (d. 1663)

Sugar and slavery

The Pennants

The Pennants stemmed from Flintshire, where in the 1480s their ancestor Thomas Pennant had rebuilt Basingwerk Abbey while its abbot. The abbot's great-grandson, Gifford, or Giffard, Pennant, a captain in the Horse, emigrated to Jamaica in 1658 and established sugar plantations in the parish of Clarendon.

The Pennants were pioneers in developing what was to become a vastly profitable industry. Sugar cane was introduced to Jamaica from Brazil by the Dutch in the 1640s. Following the final expulsion of the Spanish from Jamaica in 1660, English settlers such as the Pennants were free to concentrate on satisfying the growing European preference for sugar as a sweetener for food and in particular the newly fashionable hot drinks, tea and coffee. The success of the planters' estates depended on a large labour force of slaves, which was supplied by the Triangular

Making sugar

The sugar canes were brought to the mills by oxcarts and crushed in rollers pulled by mules or cattle, but later powered by steam. Nearby, the mashed liquor was poured into coppers for boiling and progressively reduced until it could be left to crystallise, while the molasses that ran off during cooling was converted into rum. Quicklime was added at the boiling stage as a preservative and an aid to crystallisation. The crystallised sugar and its by-products, rum and molasses, were returned to Britain in the third leg of the trade. By the mid-18th century the West Indies were the most valuable part of the British Empire and the wealth of the Jamaican planters had become proverbial.

Sir Samuel Pennant (1709–50)

Trade. Manufactured goods were exported from Britain to West Africa with which to buy slaves. The slaves were transported from there on the dreaded 'middle passage' to the West Indies, where they were employed to cut and gather the sugar canes.

Gifford Pennant's son Edward (1672–1736) extended the family estates further, becoming Chief Justice of Jamaica and a member of the governing Council. Edward Pennant's neighbours on the island at this time included Peter Beckford, a cousin and ancestor of the celebrated creator of Fonthill, and Henry Dawkins, grandfather of the builder of Penrhyn Castle.

Edward divided his estates between his sons John, Samuel and Henry Pennant. The ambition of most planters was to escape the disease and uncertain climate of the West Indies and become absentee landlords, leaving the chore of managing their estates to attorneys or foremen. Edward Pennant's sons were no different. Samuel (1709–50) departed for London in 1732 and became a partner of Messrs Drake and Long, West India Merchants, thenceforth Drake, Pennant and Long. He left the partnership in 1740 to become Common Councilman for the Cheap ward of London, and in 1742 he was elected Alderman for Bishopsgate ward. From 1744 to 1745 he served as one of the Sheriffs of London during the second Jacobite Rebellion, and for his defence of the City and his loyalty to the Hanoverian cause, he was knighted by George II in 1745. In 1749 he became Lord Mayor, but died in office the following year as a result of a virulent strain of jail-fever, contracted while presiding as a judge. Samuel Pennant's estates became the property of his brothers as 'tenants-in-common'.

John and Henry Pennant had settled in England in 1739. John became a successful merchant in Liverpool, the chief British port for the sugar trade, and in 1761 acquired his brother Henry's Jamaican property as a lifetime gift. The Pennant brothers also began acquiring property in Britain, gradually reuniting the divided Penrhyn estate in their own hands. In 1765 John Pennant's only surviving son and heir, Richard Pennant (1739–1808), married the heiress to one portion of the Penrhyn estate, Anne Susannah Warburton. Two years later the brothers bought Anne, Lady Yonge's portion, and in 1768 John was assigned the rents from that of her son, Sir George Yonge. On the death of Anne Warburton's father, General Hugh Warburton, in 1771, Richard Pennant inherited the Warburton share, which included the Penrhyn demesne, together with Winnington Hall and estate, with its lucrative salt workings, in Cheshire. When Henry died unmarried in 1772, he passed his share in Penrhyn to his brother. Thus, when John himself died in 1781, Richard Pennant was in possession of three-quarters of the estate and receiving the rents of the other quarter (Sir George Yonge's portion). In 1785 he reunited the entire estate for the first time since 1713 by purchasing the Yonge property.

(Right)
The Pennants'
Denbigh sugar
plantation in
Jamaica

Richard Pennant, improver

Richard Pennant (1739–1808) is one of the lesser known, but most impressive industrial and agrarian improvers of the later 18th century. The circumstances of his birth are obscure, as it coincided with the return of his parents, John and Bonella, from the West Indies to England; he may even have been born at sea during the voyage. He was educated at Trinity College, Cambridge, and most of his early career was spent building on his father's success as a Liverpool merchant. West Indian connections secured him the sponsorship of Alderman Beckford in entering Parliament as MP for Petersfield in Hampshire in 1761. Through the influence of his wife Anne Susannah, whose grandfather had been a Liverpool MP, he secured one of the two Liverpool seats in 1767 and held it initially until 1780, speaking often in the House, particularly on trade matters and in support of the American colonists' grievances.

When his father died in 1781, Richard had already decided on the formula for his later success, which was to apply the profits from the family's West Indian sugar plantations to the wholesale development of their Caernarfon-shire estates. The effect was not to be confined to the Penrhyn lands. In fact, his succession has been called 'the crucial turning point in the economic development of Caernarvonshire'.

Though extensive, the Penrhyn estate which Richard Pennant inherited would have seemed unpromising to many. The tortuous line of succession had led to chronic under-investment, and 'the country was scarcely passable, the roads not better than very bad horse-paths, the

(Right) Richard Pennant (1739–1808); painted by Henry Thomson. He transformed the Penrhyn estate by his agricultural improvements and developed the slate quarries. The map he points to shows the new, more direct route of the road he built via Capel Curig to Holyhead. In the background is the Royal Hotel (now Plas y Brenin) he built at Capel Curig in 1801

Anna Susannah, Lady Penrhyn (1745–1816); painted by Henry Thomson. Joint heiress to the Penrhyn estate, she married Richard Pennant in 1765

structure to a large extent, though they were revised in order to relocate the stables. He retained the cellars and the spiral stair in the north-west corner, but transformed the great hall into a symmetrical entrance hall, and added turrets and crenellations and a further wing of family rooms at the south-east. The house was built in a curious form of castellated Gothic, and what struck most visitors was its colour, resulting from hanging 'mathematical' tiles on the walls, which gave the appearance of yellow brick. 'Penrhyn glitters in its yellow glory', wrote a visitor in 1791, 'beautifully contrasted with the pure white of the interspersed cottages of the plain.'

In 1786 another brother, Benjamin Wyatt (1745–1818) was appointed general agent to the estate, which he remained until 1817. Though the agricultural character of his native Staffordshire was quite different, he quickly identified the main deficiencies of farming on the predominantly mountainous estate. His remedies were the provision of shelter and winter fodder. Shelter came either in the form of new buildings (which he designed himself) or from plantations. By 1800 it was estimated that 600,000 trees had been planted on the estate, and the improvement of the farmland was accelerated by drainage and manuring. Wyatt introduced turnips and scotch cabbage for fodder, and encouraged crop rotation. In 1789 all the farm leases were renewed with printed documents including clauses on correct husbandry.

cottages wretched, the farmers poor'. Pennant's collaborators in bringing about his revolution were members of the ingenious Wyatt family of Staffordshire, which from the mid 18th century produced 28 architects and a dynasty of outstanding land agents, who served the Penrhyn estate for a hundred years from 1786.

The Wyatts

Pennant had employed the most famous Wyatt, James, in adding a wing to Winnington Hall in 1776, but at Penrhyn it was to his brother Samuel (1737–1807) that he turned to modernise the ancient hall-house he had inherited. Wyatt's designs respected the earlier

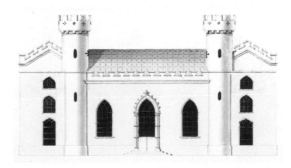

The west front of Penrhyn as remodelled by Samuel Wyatt after 1782

Slate

It was slate that was to transform the fortunes of Richard Pennant and Penrhyn. The word 'slate' is related to the French *esclater*, meaning 'to break into pieces', for it has the unusual geological property that it can be split cleanly into thin but strong sheets of almost any size, which make an ideal roofing material. Slate is found in much of north-west Wales and had been extracted from the mountain at Cae Braich y Cafn at the north end of the Nant Ffrancon valley since at least the 15th century, but the remoteness of the region and the lack of good roads meant that it had remained a largely local activity. By the 1760s quarrying was still on a very small scale, with dozens of workings being exploited by as many individuals. In 1765 General Warburton's agent, Mr Hughes, decided to lease the quarry workings to about 80 of them, at an annual rent of one pound.

Very soon after he succeeded, Richard Pennant called in these leases and took the management of the quarry in hand. He removed quantities of overburden and slate waste, and built a new road from the quarry to the mouth of the River Cegin, later to be extended south down the Nant Ffrancon, and through the Ogwen valley to Capel Curig. On his arrival he found that the quarry could muster only four carts for the carriage of the slate, and by engaging farm tenants and labourers in the work he increased this to 100. At the river mouth he established Port (or Porth) Penrhyn from 1786.

Shugborough was entirely clad in Penrhyn slate

Here, the slates were embarked for shipment to other parts of Britain and Ireland.

Richard Pennant's reforms and later mechanisation greatly increased the output of the quarry, but the work of the quarrymen remained fundamentally unchanged. A slate block had first to be detached from the quarry face, by wedges and later explosive charges, inserted by men often dangling on ropes over precipitous drops. The detached blocks were then cleaved and divided ('pillared') into smaller blocks, and finally split and dressed by hand in sheds some distance away.

The Wyatts played a leading role in the marketing of the slate. In 1801 Lord Penrhyn (as he had by then become) signed an agreement with Samuel Worthington, Michael Humble and Samuel Holland, all of Liverpool, by which these individuals were to be supplied with all the slates from Penrhyn quarry at specified rates '… excepting all such slates as Samuel Wyatt or James Wyatt of London, architects, shall or may want within business respectively'. Samuel used it for the fittings of the new stables at Holkham, Norfolk, and seems to have taken a positive interest in extending the range of its use, for shelves, cisterns, lavatory seats and window-sills. At Shugborough he clad the entire house in squared Penrhyn slates painted to resemble ashlar (squared stone), and constructed a portico of columns constructed of thin fillets of slate around a wooden core.

The smoothness of properly split and ground slate makes it an ideal writing surface, from which marks in chalk can be easily erased. The gradual spread of education to all classes from the later 18th century, in which Pennant himself played a part as a builder of schools, created an enormous demand for 'blackboards' large and small that he sought to satisfy. On the wharf at Port Penrhyn, a manufactory was established for the finishing and framing of writing-slates. 'Previously, we were entirely supplied from Switzerland', wrote Thomas Pennant, but 'that trade has now ceased; the Swiss manufacturers are become bankrupt.' Every year 136,000 writing slates were produced at Port Penrhyn, consuming 3,000 feet of timber for the frames, and employing up to 30 men.

The growth of mass education in the 19th century depended on Penrhyn writing slates

Complementary enterprises

In 1783 Pennant was created Baron Penrhyn of Penrhyn, County Louth, an Irish title which did not prevent him from sitting as a member of the Commons. (To avoid confusion with Edward Gordon, 1st Lord Penrhyn of Llandegai, he is here referred to as Richard Pennant throughout.) From 1784 to 1790 he again represented Liverpool and in that time made 30 speeches, all on the Liverpool trade and the West Indies, leading the planters' defence of the slave trade with such vigour that he was known as the 'Chairman of the West Indian Merchants'.

Richard Pennant never visited Jamaica, but kept in close touch with his representatives on the island. He was particularly adept at devising new variations to the reciprocal Triangular Trade, upon which the success of the West Indian sugar industry depended. In 1782, he was writing to Jamaica offering 'Mechanicks … Carpenters, Smiths, Coopers, Bricklayers, etc, etc', and, remarkably, the slaves developed a partiality to herrings shipped from Britain. Manure was also sent on the returning ships, and Pennant, the true entrepreneur, was alive to the prospects for diversification. He had the foresight to predict the importance of cotton many years before it replaced sugar as the most important crop traded across the Atlantic.

This talent for complementary enterprises led to a number of mutually supporting activities on the Caernarfonshire estate. The leading figure in most of these was Samuel Worthington, the merchant with whom Pennant signed an agreement in 1796 allowing him to search for minerals on the estate. Worthington found manganese and zinc ores (for bleaching and pigments respectively), ochre (also for pigments) and extracted chert and quartz from the base of Carnedd Llywelyn near the slate quarry. With flints shipped on the slate vessels returning from Ireland, these materials were processed for the ceramic industry at a mill on the River Ogwen, and kilns by the port. Their principal destination was the Herculaneum pottery in Liverpool, in which Messrs Humble and Holland, the distributors of the Penrhyn slate, were founding partners.

The principal product continued to be slate, and the combined energies of Richard Pennant and Benjamin Wyatt were irresistible, despite the most adverse conditions. When war broke out against France in 1793, and the Prime Minister, William Pitt, imposed a crippling tax on all slate carried coastwise, the workforce at the quarry slumped from six hundred to a little over one hundred. 'The spirit of building', which had fuelled the demand for slate over the past decade, was broken, said the Penrhyn 'slate reeve' (or foreman), William Williams. The redundant quarrymen were pressed into service in a new venture, the creation of an iron tramway from the quarry to the port, 6¼ miles long and falling through 500 feet. Work was put in hand to deepen the port itself to enable it to take larger vessels, once the trade recovered. The tramway, which was to operate from 1801 until replaced by a steam railway in 1874, vastly increased the efficiency and capacity of the operation in the early decades of the 19th century; 12 men and 16 horses could now transport a greater annual quantity to the port than 140 men with 400 horses had done before the tramway was built. At the same time, William Williams set about the excavation of proper working 'galleries' in the quarry faces.

Building at Penrhyn

Whilst the building trade at large was supplied with ever-increasing quantities of Penrhyn slate, Pennant and the Wyatts were themselves building on a considerable scale. Samuel Wyatt designed a classical villa near the port known as 'Lime Grove' for the agent to the estate; his brother Benjamin, who held that post from 1786, acted as architect for a whole series of buildings which, while perhaps less sophisticated, were none the less both useful and delightful. Soon after his appointment Benjamin Wyatt designed a Neo-classical cattle shed in the park, complete with a Doric colonnade, and a dairy farm near the quarry at Penisa'rnant, which combined the Neo-classical and Gothic styles. Equipped with cool slate slabs and furnished with Wedgwood pottery, the dairy was surrounded by a pleasure ground, whose ornaments included 'a small stool made to imitate a giant mushroom. An apiary well contrived with straw hive and glass one [*sic*]: at the back of the house ... a curious piggery and poultry yard, with a fountain playing in one of the courts.' A tunnel was built under the new road so that the pigs could reach the mountain pasture.

Where the newly created parkland touched the sea, between the mouths of the rivers Ogwen and Cegin, Benjamin Wyatt built a splendid marine bath for bathing in heated sea water, at the end of an 'artifical mole'. 'There is a dressing room each side, or rather an undressing room, one for the ladies and the other for the gentlemen.' The route to the baths from the castle, 'by an amazing high carriage terrace', became an important feature of the park, much enjoyed by visitors, who could rest on the way at 'an elegant little cottage of her ladyship ... overun [*sic*] with Passion flowers and beautiful creepers of various kinds' and which included a room decorated with caricature prints.

To the tourist influenced by contemporary Romanticism, the great industrial ventures of the late 18th century became almost as important destinations as the Sublime scenery of mountains and valleys. Penrhyn had both industry and landscape, and Pennant and Wyatt were quick to cater for this new interest. They built a new hotel at Capel Curig for visitors to Snowdon, and another by Port Penrhyn, the Penrhyn Arms, for visitors to the castle and the quarry.

Sadly, little of Richard Pennant's built legacy remains. Only his monument, by Richard Westmacott, set up at his widow's instigation in Llandegai church in 1821, does justice to his achievements. It consists of a sarcophagus, flanked by heroic figures of a quarryman and a peasant girl with her distaff, and with a frieze of four groups of putti, emblematic of the state of the country before his succession, and his improvements in slate quarrying, education and agriculture.

Lady Penrhyn survived her husband by eight years, and continued to live at Penrhyn. Their marriage was childless, and so her husband left the property on his death in 1808 to his cousin, George Hay Dawkins, although for her lifetime she enjoyed the income from the quarry. Lord Penrhyn's will provided annuities to her lady's maid for the welfare of her ladyship's three pug dogs and to the groom for the care of seven horses and seven dogs.

(Right) Lime Grove was a classical villa built by Samuel Wyatt near the port for the agent to the estate

Building the castle

The client:
George Hay Dawkins-Pennant

George Hay Dawkins (1764–1840) took up his inheritance on the death of Lady Penrhyn in 1816, assuming the additional name and arms of Pennant in accordance with his benefactor's will. He was the second son of Henry Dawkins II of Standlynch, Wiltshire, and of Over Norton, Oxfordshire, and his wife Lady Juliana Colyear, daughter of the 2nd Earl of Portmore. Dawkins was also the great-great-grandson of Gifford Pennant of Jamaica. His first wife, the Hon. Sophia Mary Maude, bore him two daughters but probably never set eyes on Penrhyn. She died at the age of 40, after only five years of marriage, in 1812. Two years later Dawkins married Elizabeth, daughter of the Hon. William Henry Bouverie, brother of the 2nd Earl of Radnor.

It is tantalising that we know so little of the life of a man who could call into being so fantastic and original a building as Penrhyn Castle. Like his benefactor before him, he was a Member of Parliament, for Newark in Nottinghamshire in 1814–18 and New Romney in Kent in 1820–30. From the little evidence that does survive, he comes across as a reserved, almost austere, character, driven by what the German traveller and horticulturalist Prince Herman von Pückler-Muskau, visiting Penrhyn during its construction, described as 'buildingmania … this wealthy man lives with his family in a humble cottage in the neighbourhood, with a small establishment; he feasts once a week on the sight of his

fairy castle, which, after the long continuation of such simple habits, he will probably never bring himself to inhabit. It appeared to give him great pleasure to show and explain everything to me, and I experienced no less from his enthusiasm, which was agreeable and becoming in a man otherwise cold.'

In Parliament Dawkins-Pennant consistently opposed the movement for reform of the electoral system that led to the Great Reform Bill of 1832, and the emancipation of slaves within the British Empire. (He received compensation of £14,683 for the 764 slaves on his estates, when this measure was effected in 1833.)

(Right) George Hay Dawkins-Pennant (1764–1840), the builder of the castle; painted by John Jackson

(Above) An early design for Dawkins-Pennant's new castle

Dawkins-Pennant moved to Penrhyn the year after Waterloo had put an end to two decades of war. He had had eight years in which to contemplate improvements. As the result of the war and its taxes, unemployment and destitution were serious problems in Caernarfonshire, as elsewhere. In 1818 for the first time a nightly patrol had to be established in Bangor for the control of vagrants, and the Select Committee on Telford's Holyhead Road urged that the work be accelerated, both to take advantage of cheap labour and for the sake of employing the large numbers out of work. It is not hard to imagine Dawkins-Pennant seeing an opportunity as well as a duty in this situation.

However, to see the building of Penrhyn Castle merely as an exercise in job-creation would be absurd, for there were a number of other influences that must have borne on Dawkins-Pennant at this time. The house he had inherited in 1808 was still barely 30 years old, and not insubstantial, but if in 1798 it could have been faintly praised as 'a good specimen of the military Gothic', it was now fast becoming unfashionable. Meanwhile, along the coast at Abergele, Lloyd Bamford Hesketh had been building himself a castle called Gwrych, in many ways the most successful Picturesque building of all.

Pückler-Muskau was one of those who witnessed the building of the new Penrhyn Castle, and in his astonishment at the scale of the enterprise he mused on the castles of William the Conqueror's time: 'What could then be accomplished only by a mighty monarch is now executed, as a plaything, – only with increased size, magnificence and expense, – by a simple country-gentleman, whose father very likely sold cheeses'.

In one major respect he was wrong. Dawkins-Pennant's father had owned a substantial country house that had been bought by the nation for the descendants of Lord Nelson; his aunt, Lady Caroline Colyear, had married the 1st Lord Scarsdale, builder of Kedleston Hall in Derbyshire, and his uncle, James Dawkins, had led the expedition that rediscovered the ruined cities of Baalbec and Palmyra in 1751. The selling of cheeses did not figure in this pedigree. On the contrary, the fusion of these elements – antiquarianism, architectural patronage on the grand scale, two West Indian fortunes and a burgeoning agricultural estate and industrial enterprise – was tantamount to alchemy.

49

The architect: Thomas Hopper

It is not clear how Dawkins-Pennant came to appoint Thomas Hopper (1776–1856) as his architect; prior to Penrhyn (and Gosford, Co. Armagh, begun slightly earlier), his country-house work had been confined to remodellings and alterations. His most significant commission by far had been the construction of a new conservatory for the Prince of Wales at Carlton House in London in 1807, a fantasia on the chapel of Henry VII in Westminster Abbey, replete with ancient Welsh heraldry and vaulted in cast iron.

In October 1817 an unremarkable payment is recorded in Dawkins-Pennant's Cash Book: 'John Williams Coachman, for a Xmas box' – five shillings. Curiously, the following May there occurs the further entry: 'To John Williams, Coachman of the Prince Regent, a Xmas box', again five shillings. Williams was similarly rewarded (and described) in July 1820, by which time work was proceeding on the new castle. If Williams actually brought the Prince to Penrhyn at these times, the recommendation of

Thomas Hopper must have come with him.

It seems unlikely that Hopper was responsible for the two anonymous proposal drawings that survive, one for a great hall and the other a perspective from the south west. Although the perspective prefigures the shape of the principal block, and the hall design shows some of the devices later employed by Hopper, the drawings have none of the boldness and assurance of his executed work, and must represent a rejected proposal by a lesser architect.

What must be by Hopper is a single, unsigned plan inscribed 'Ground Plan of Penrhyn Castle/ Dawkins Pennant Esqre', but not dated. Most of this plan was adopted; the major differences lie at the northern end of the west front, where a massive square block with circular towers at the corners was proposed, containing on one side a 'Great Drawing Room' 76 by 36 feet and lit by five windows facing south. Even at Penrhyn this would have been a prodigious room, and it is not known whether it was ever begun, but its omission may explain the somewhat inarticulate appearance of this elevation today. Hopper certainly lived up to his famous dictum that 'it is an architect's business to understand all styles and to be prejudiced in favour of none', but the reasons for the choice of the 'Norman' style at Penrhyn are not obvious. Whereas at Gosford, Co. Armagh, where Hopper also began a new castle in 1820, the Norman style must have seemed the obvious choice in an Ireland conquered by Strongbow, in North Wales the conquerors' style was the late 13th-century Gothic of the great royal castles built by the Plantagenet Edward I at Caernarfon and Conwy. Here, perhaps, an 'earlier' style was deliberately used 'to suggest a more ancient, and therefore native, lineage'.

Constructing Penrhyn

In April 1819 William Baxter, 'who superintends the works carrying on at Penrhyn Castle', was sent to Penmon on Anglesey to agree prices for stone from a number of quarries around the promontory. The work began with the construction of a new park wall, seven miles in circuit, which displaced six farms and the main road, which Dawkins-Pennant re-routed. The wall was built of rubble stones from the Cochwillan and other quarries, and topped with a coping of rough Penrhyn blue slate slabs laid on edge. The Grand Lodge was begun, possibly by the masons recently employed on Lord Anglesey's column at Llanfairpwll, and the massive gates hung. Yards for the carpenters and masons were established (where the disabled car-park is today) and by July 1819 the carpenters were at work, presumably preparing the scaffolding. The walls of the new castle were probably rising by 1821.

For the next few years the accounts fall silent, but by October 1826 the Library Tower, the Oak Tower and the Grand Hall were all completed and were being slated. A drawing of this date by Dawkins-Pennant's eighteen-year-old daughter, Juliana, shows no sign of the Keep. While the works were in progress, she went on a sketching tour which took in Warwick Castle (where she drew Guy's Tower), and Charlecote church. Two years later, Pückler-Muskau was shown the 'eating hall' (the Grand Hall), by the architect himself, and was able to describe many of the out-offices, in particular the laundry. The plasterers were on site by the spring of 1830, when 400 bushels of cow hair were delivered, and lime was brought from the kilns at Port Penrhyn. In June and July 292 polished plates

of glass arrived from the Ravenshead works of J. Crockford & Co., and from a drawing dated 9 October, it appears that the Keep and the other principal towers had risen to their full height. The drawing shows the outline of the stables in a dotted line, and these clearly constituted the last major phase of work, between August 1831 and June 1833. When the thirteen-year-old Princess Victoria visited in 1832, she found the castle 'not near finished yet', and although the number of visitors rose dramatically from 1833, the furnishings were not yet complete in the early months of 1835, when Hopper was still preoccupied with candelabra and other fittings.

Throughout the building period, there are large numbers of accounts for building stone, from the Anglesey limestone quarries around Penmon, Red Wharf Bay and Moelfre, to an almost equally large number of suppliers. The external walling is of Penmon limestone, a dark grey or black stone with many large fossils and other defects. In view of these drawbacks, the exceptionally fine jointing speaks highly of the master masons, of whom Nathan Ryan, Griff Jones and William Pritchard are named in the accounts. From the frequency and size of his payments on account, one Edward Jones of Llandygai appears to have been the principal contractor.

(Far left) Thomas Hopper (1776–1856), the architect of the castle

(Right) The west front

The craftsmen of Penrhyn

Chimneypieces were supplied by Thomas Crisp in 1833–4. The name of the master plasterer has not emerged, but the work is of such high quality that the firm of the leading plaster craftsman of the day, Francis Bernasconi, has been suggested. Robert Offer, a native of Bath who died at Bangor in 1829 and was described as 'many years foreman of the plasterers at Penrhyn Castle', may not have been responsible for the ornamental work.

Penrhyn Castle can be seen as the masterpiece of the stonemasons and carpenters of North Wales in any period. 'Mr Pennant deserves the thanks and admiration of every friend of Wales', wrote Angharad Llwyd in 1832, 'for the almost exclusive encouragement he has given to the native artificers of every kind …', and Adela Douglas-Pennant later wrote that 'the entire work was carried out by local workmen under the superintendence of the architect Mr

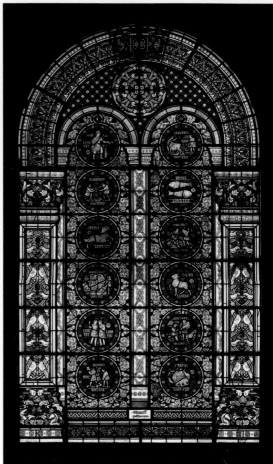

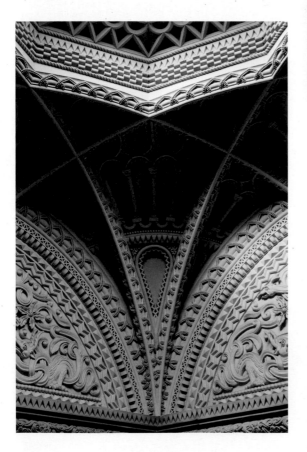

Hopper'. She adds that most of the Norman furniture was made by the estate carpenters. The fact that none of the oak columns, the dadoes and the neo-Norman furniture is carved from the solid, but rather composed of applied, pre-carved, repeated elements gives credence to this claim. Taken together, this combination on the grandest scale of Welsh oak, limestone, slate and marble shaped by 'native skill' can be seen as the expression of pride in the raw materials of his adopted region by a rich squire who was also a prodigious 'extractor'.

Hopper employed not only local craftsmen, but in Thomas Willement the leading stained-glass designer in Britain. Willement supplied superb glass, featuring the signs of the zodiac, for the Grand Hall, and may have provided designs for the decoration of the Dining Room. As

Heraldic Artist to George IV, he must surely have had a say in the heraldic programme as a whole, but, surprisingly, he was not asked to supply armorial glass; that was provided by David Evans of Shrewsbury.

The total cost of the work is not recorded, and early estimates varied considerably. It can, however, hardly have been less than the £123,000 suggested by Catherine Sinclair, who describes Penrhyn in her book *Hill and Valley* (1839). Money was certainly not a problem for Dawkins-Pennant. At his death in 1840, his income was estimated at £80,000 per annum, and his personal property 'sworn under £600,000'.

Picturesque and sublime

Penrhyn is to such an extent unique that it has persistently defied description or categorisation. 'To wander through the wondrous halls of Penrhyn', wrote Louisa Stuart Costello in 1845, 'is like struggling along in a bewildered dream occasioned by having studied some elaborate work on the early buildings of the Saxons or Normans.' To early visitors, whether they thought it 'Saxon', 'Norman', 'Roman', or 'one of the most complete castellated baronial mansions in the kingdom', Penrhyn was never unimpressive, and always counted a success. Though Hopper's building would not for an instant deceive anyone with an idea of what a Norman castle actually looked like, in his compilation of architectural types and decorative elements spanning at least three medieval centuries, he produced a castle that was at once more 'archaeological' than its near-contemporaries, and yet eminently Picturesque. Of course, the site was exceptional, and ancient, but the distant view of the clear and commanding outline of the Keep suggests a strategic importance it never had.

In all its massiveness, Penrhyn partakes of the Romantic notion of the Sublime, the infinite or immeasurable, perhaps best appreciated at the foot of the Keep. Most importantly, despite the necessity for adequate windows in place of loopholes and arrow slits, the castle also looks defensible. No other late Georgian castle-builders went to such trouble in this respect; most would have been content, for example, with conventional – perhaps mildly Gothicised – stables, where Hopper and Dawkins-Pennant threw up a high curtain wall with four titanic towers complete with 'murder holes'. Penrhyn was a genuinely secure fortress; secure also, therefore, from Pugin's famous swipe at modern castles: 'who would hammer against nailed portals', he asked in 1841, 'when he could kick his way through the greenhouse?' Whether the fortification of Penrhyn was due simply to a desire for historical accuracy or to actual fears of a possible siege is a matter for speculation.

(Left, top) Willement stained glass in the Grand Hall

(Far left) The plasterwork ceiling of the Grand Staircase

(Right) The north front in 1846; lithography by G. Hawkins

Technology

The choice of an exotic style like Norman Gothic presented architects with formidable technical challenges, not the least of which was the placing of chimneys. At Penrhyn, with 70 roofs of sharply differing heights, Hopper was forced to distribute the smoke from his fireplaces by the most tortuous and unlikely routes (no fewer than seventeen flues converge in the upper storeys of the Housemaids' Tower, for instance), but in some respects he was able to draw on new technology. The ducted hot-air system which heated the Grand Hall and neighbouring rooms was among the first to be installed in mainland Britain.

(Right) The Drawing Room candelabra were originally lit by oil

Piped water was a rarer luxury. Miss Sinclair writes that 'in each dressing-room, instead of a window-seat, a bath is placed, with pipes of hot and cold water perpetually ready…. It is to be hoped that the progress of luxury and comfort will at last introduce this indulgence into every house and dressing-room in England.' Water-closets were lavishly provided, some of them on the upper floors spectacularly top-lit by lofty skylights or lanterns.

Lighting was at first by oil; gas fittings were subsequently installed, which were replaced with electricity in 1927–8 by A.V. Gifkins & Co. of Victoria St, Westminster. Most of the bronze lamps are of the type named after the Swiss inventor Aimé Argand, and they were not uncommon in British houses by the 1820s.

Sources

The pursuit of sources for the design of the castle, its interiors and furnishings, may never end. There seems little doubt, however, that the

(Left) A plate showing details from Shireburn Minster, Dorset, taken from John Carter's Ancient Architecture of England, which inspired much of the decoration at Penrhyn

Keep is derived from that of Hedingham Castle in Essex, where Hopper served as County Surveyor for 40 years. In the arrangements of the towers, and particularly the northern (entrance) elevation of the stable block, there are close similarities with Raglan Castle in Gwent. Among more recent castles, Eastnor in Herefordshire (by Robert Smirke, c.1812–20), despite its basic symmetry, prefigures Penrhyn in the play of square and round towers, and especially in the use of tall, round towers leading the eye round each angle.

For the interior, medieval precedents are less easy to find for the architecture than for the decoration, even in the case of the Grand Hall (sometimes compared with the nave of Durham Cathedral). For precedents in the revived Norman style, one authority has proposed a volume of stage designs for the Berlin Theatre by Karl Schinkel, published in 1819–24.

Perhaps closer still, since they actually show domestic interiors in the Norman style, are the unexecuted designs for Lea Castle, Worcestershire, by John Carter, produced a year before his death in 1818. An unsuccessful architect, Carter made his name as a draughtsman and engraver of medieval buildings and their decoration. His masterpiece was *The Ancient Architecture of England* (1795–1814), a compendium of engraved plates of details mainly from ecclesiastical buildings, which has as much of the character of a pattern-book as a purely antiquarian treatise. It was almost certainly a major source of designs for the decoration of columns, capitals, arches and doorways at Penrhyn (Dawkins-Pennant's own copy survives in the Library).

Dawkins-Pennant indulged to the full Hopper's considerable ingenuity in designing new furniture and carpets in a 'Norman' style. For, surprisingly, he seems not to have shared the passion for collecting 'baronial' furniture and fittings that affected many other castle-builders of the time. He died in December 1840, only a few years after his castle was completed, and was buried in the Dawkins family vault at Chipping Norton in Oxfordshire.

One book that was unquestionably drawn upon was **Joseph Strutt's** *Sports and Pastimes of the English People* (1801), a scholarly survey of the popular recreations of 'Olden Time' with illustrations chiefly taken from the margins of medieval manuscripts. Many of these were copied directly for the carved decoration at Penrhyn. Strutt's work also provided valuable source material for Sir Walter Scott's *Ivanhoe*, published in 1820, the year Penrhyn was begun. Scott and Hopper faced similar difficulties in reconstructing the Middle Ages, and just as the dialogue in *Ivanhoe* was not written 'in Anglo-Saxon or in Norman French', Hopper allowed his castle the anachronisms of fitted carpets, water closets and plate glass.

The Douglas-Pennants of Penrhyn

Edward Gordon Douglas-Pennant, 1st Lord Penrhyn

George Dawkins-Pennant had no children by his second marriage, and so his two daughters (known as the 'Slate Queens', or the Queen of Diamonds and the Queen of Hearts) were his heirs. The elder, Juliana Isabella Mary, who inherited Penrhyn, was married in 1833 to Edward Gordon Douglas (1800–86), captain in the Grenadier Guards, and grandson of the 14th Earl of Morton; he was promoted colonel the following year. According to his youngest daughter, Adela, this younger-son-of-a-

Edward Gordon Douglas-Pennant, 1st Baron Penrhyn (1800–86); painted by Eden Eddis

The royal visit in 1859

'A man was specially had down from Miller's the great lamp shop in London, to see after the lighting of the house during the Royal visit, instead of trusting to the services of the ordinary "lamp man" of the House. This man deserted his duties, to see the arrival of the Royal guests and omitted to light the corkscrew staircase up to the keep, so that when my mother took the Queen to her room, she found the stairs in complete darkness. My Mother begged the Queen to wait while she ran upstairs for a light, but on returning to the head of the steps, she found the Queen had laughingly groped her way up behind her in the dark.'

Adela Douglas-Pennant

younger-son hesitated to propose to so great an heiress, but was encouraged by Mrs Dawkins-Pennant, who was his first cousin. Her husband seems to have found the idea not to his liking, and after a stormy interview, Capt. Douglas removed himself and his luggage to the Penrhyn Arms Hotel. The marriage eventually took place at St Marylebone, and 150 workmen sat down to supper in their honour at Port Penrhyn, consuming 473 quarts of ale in the process. The couple lived in Yorkshire until Dawkins-Pennant's death in 1840.

In 1841, in accordance with Dawkins-Pennant's will, they became the Hon. Edward and Mrs Douglas-Pennant, and in that year Col. Douglas-Pennant was elected as MP for Carnarvonshire (which he continued to represent until elevated to the peerage in 1866). The following winter, Juliana caught a chill while climbing Snowdon, having lent her cloak to another of the party. The ailment worsened, and on medical advice the family set out for the Riviera to effect a cure. Juliana caught a fresh chill at Pisa and died there in April 1842.

Juliana Isabella Dawkins-Pennant (1808–42); miniature by Adam Buck. The heiress to the Penrhyn estate, she married Edward Douglas in 1833

In 1846 Col. Douglas-Pennant took as his second wife Lady Maria Louisa Fitzroy, daughter of the 5th Duke of Grafton, having met her hunting at his Northamptonshire seat, Wicken Park (which he had leased from the Mordaunt family in 1840 and later bought). Douglas-Pennant and his family lived at Penrhyn for only part of the year, generally residing there principally in August and from October to Christmas. The rest of the year was spent at Wicken and at Mortimer House in Halkin Street, Belgravia, the family's London home from 1859. The family's whereabouts dictated the hours during which the castle was opened to the public (tickets were sold at the Penrhyn Arms and other local hotels).

Col. Douglas-Pennant added greatly to the Penrhyn estate (see p. 63), especially in the Meillonydd district of the Llŷn Peninsula, and to the collection of pictures. In 1859 he entertained the Queen and Prince Albert at the castle. They planted trees in the grounds, toured the Nant Ffrancon valley and the slate quarry, and after dinner at the castle heard the Llanllechid choir sing choruses from the *Messiah* in Welsh in the Grand Hall.

Col. Douglas-Pennant was created 1st Baron Penrhyn of Llandegai in 1866. Never a frequent speaker in either House, none the less he was constantly busy in committees. He was well acquainted with Gladstone, and their political differences did not prevent Mrs Gladstone's frequent presence at Penrhyn, for the families had much in common. Gladstone's father had been a Liverpool merchant who owned substan-

tial sugar plantations in the West Indies. Like Lord Penrhyn's father-in-law, Gladstone had begun his political career as MP for Newark and in his maiden speech in 1833 he had stoutly defended the West Indian interest. The Gladstones habitually spent a month's holiday along the coast at Penmaenmawr, and while staying there in September 1861, they spent a few nights at Penrhyn.

More remarkable was Col. Douglas-Pennant's friendship with prominent local politicians such as John Morgan, owner of a small factory at Cadnant, a Welsh radical and editor of a Welsh newspaper whose opinions Adela Douglas-Pennant described as 'advanced'. Her father was prominent in public works: he gave land for schools and churches, improved the Bangor infirmary, and contributed to the restoration of Bangor Cathedral. His restoration of the parish church at Llandygai may have had more to do with landscape improvements, since the tower became a feature in the principal distant views of the castle.

When Col. Douglas-Pennant was raised to the peerage in 1866, his son, George Sholto, succeeded him as MP for Carnarvonshire. When the seat was next contested, in 1868, George Sholto was defeated by T. L. D. Jones-Parry, a Liberal, the son of a Bethesda quarryman but himself a young professional with diverse business interests. This event is perhaps symbolic of the passing not only of an era in Caernarfonshire politics but of the old order of the paternalistic landlord in the county.

Lady Maria Louisa Fitzroy (1818–1912) was the 1st Lord Penrhyn's second wife

2nd Lord Penrhyn

George Sholto Douglas-Pennant was born in 1836 and educated at Eton and Oxford. As a young man he travelled in Egypt, Syria, the Holy Land and the Balkans, and in America he is said to have witnessed Blondin's tightrope walk across Niagara. Returning from his travels in 1860 he married Pamela Rushout, daughter of Sir Charles Rushout of Sezincote in Gloucestershire. She bore him seven children, and they were a devoted couple. Her death only nine years after their marriage threw him into a decline, which was only arrested by two further years abroad in the early 1870s, collecting curiosities and corresponding regularly with his young family. In 1875 his recovery was completed by his marriage to Gertrude Jessy Glynne, a niece of Mrs Gladstone; Jessy is said to have reminded him of his first wife.

George Sholto succeeded as 2nd Baron Penrhyn on his father's death in 1886. He had assumed the ownership of the quarry a year earlier, and his reign is chiefly remembered for the great strike of 1900–3 (see p.64). The 2nd

(see p.64)

Devoted to the rod

'Fond as he is of silk and scarlet, he is, perhaps, more devoted to his 'rod' than any other sport, for in early spring and late autumn he never fails to spend a few weeks on Dee side, and until he succeeded to the cares as well as the houses of the title and estate, he was an annual visitor to Norway … The 12th finds him on his Welsh moors, whence nothing can lure him till the saddling bell at Doncaster sends forth its Leger clang.'

Bailey's *Monthly Magazine of Sports and Pastimes*, 1888

Baron maintained an interest in archaeology throughout his life, probably acquiring for the castle the stone figure of Osiris. He subscribed to the publications of his first cousin Augustus Lane-Fox (later known as General Pitt-Rivers), and was also a keen naturalist. His patronage of the firm of Morris & Co., whose wallpapers and fabrics were ordered for the Keep bedrooms in the 1890s, reveals another facet of his complex personality. The numerous racing trophies in the castle are evidence of the 2nd Baron's success as a breeder and trainer of racehorses, both at Penrhyn and at Exton in Lincolnshire. Like his father and his son, he was an active Master of the Grafton Hunt.

Lord Penrhyn's family was large and spread over a wide range of ages. Among the daughters of his first marriage were the artistically inclined Alice, who published a catalogue of the family pictures in 1902, and was renowned for her prowess at skating, and at swimming in Samuel Wyatt's Marine Bath; Hilda, a close friend of Lady Ottoline Morrell; and Violet, who worked as First Insurance Commissioner for Wales under Lloyd George, and later commanded the WRAF during the Second World War.

(Left) George Sholto Douglas-Pennant, 2nd Lord Penrhyn (1836–1907); painted by Barbara Leighton

(Right) The 2nd Lord Penrhyn laid on lavish hospitality for the Prince of Wales's visit in 1894

The 20th century

When the 2nd Baron died in 1907, he was succeeded by his eldest son, Edward Sholto Douglas-Pennant, 3rd Lord Penrhyn (1864–1927). He had met his wife, Hon. Blanche Fitzroy, at Wicken, and as an asthmatic she greatly preferred the climate there to the maritime air at Penrhyn. Edward Sholto was MP for Southern Northamptonshire from 1895 to 1900, and subsequently spent some time living at Glan Conway, the house his grand-father had bought as a shooting lodge on the Ysbyty Ifan estate.

In the First World War, Lord Penrhyn's eldest son and heir, Alan George Sholto Douglas-Pennant, and his two half brothers – children of his father's second marriage – George and Charles, were all killed in action. After the war, Lord Penrhyn lived at Wicken, which he left to his widow on his death in 1927.

His only surviving son, Hugh Napier Douglas-Pennant, succeeded him as 4th Baron. In 1922 he had married Hon. Sybil Mary, daughter of the 3rd Viscount Hardinge (the marriage was dissolved in 1941, and Lady

Edward Sholto, 3rd Lord Penrhyn (1864–1927) in the garden at Penrhyn

Saved for the nation

Like many other country houses, Penrhyn was pressed into unlikely service during the Second World War. On 23 August 1939, after months of careful preparation, the National Gallery's collection of Old Masters was evacuated from London to Aberystwyth, Bangor and Penrhyn to be beyond the range of enemy bombers. Penrhyn was chosen because it was one of the few buildings in Wales with doors large enough to admit the biggest of the National Gallery's paintings, Van Dyck's equestrian portrait of Charles I (illustrated here). The pictures were stored in the Dining Room and two coach-houses, but this refuge proved only temporary. The fall of France in 1940 increased the threat of bombing, and it was thought safer to move the collection underground to a slate mine at Blaenau Ffestiniog. From 1940 to 1945 the castle was the headquarters of the Daimler motor company. At the same time (1940–3) the BBC's variety department occupied a hall in Bangor built in the 1860s for the coming-of-age of the 2nd Lord Penrhyn. Arthur Askey, Kenneth Horne, and Tommy Handley's *ITMA* were all broadcast from here.

Penrhyn later remarried). She was a cousin of the Hon. C.S. Rolls, and it was at her instigation that in 1936 Lord Penrhyn acquired the Rolls-Royce that still belongs to the family. Their time at Penrhyn is remembered as a golden age of entertaining and weekend house-parties. Although they had no children, the many grandchildren of the 3rd Baron were frequent visitors, and Lady Penrhyn furnished the rooms with comfortable sofas and cut flowers to overcome the exaggerated formality of the Victorian age. Lord Penrhyn was Lord Lieutenant of Carnarvonshire from 1933 to 1941.

In 1949, the 4th Lord Penrhyn left Penrhyn Castle to his niece, Lady Janet Marcia Rose Harper (née Pelham), and the title became separate. Frank Douglas-Pennant, 5th Baron, is noted for having won the 1908 Grand National with the 66–1 outsider, Rubio, which had seen service between the shafts of a hotel omnibus at Towcester, and for having made his maiden speech in the House of Lords at the age of 102 in 1967.

In respect of her uncle's will, Lady Janet and her husband, Mr John Charles Harper, assumed the surname and arms of Douglas Pennant. They lived in Penrhyn for a few months only in 1949, then moved to the agent's house, and subsequently to a new house nearby. In 1951, Penrhyn Castle and the Ysbyty Ifan and Carneddau estates (except for Glan Conway House and two farms) were accepted by the Inland Revenue under the then National Land Fund procedures, and transferred to the National Trust. Lady Janet and her husband continued to be closely involved with the castle and the Trust's work there. Following the death of Lady Janet in 1997, Richard Douglas Pennant, her son, inherited the estate, and, once again in lieu of death-duties, the Trust acquired further paintings, furniture and silver gilt.

The estate since 1808

From Richard Pennant's firm foundations, the Penrhyn Estate grew in size and influence in all its departments in the 19th century. By 1893 it included 72,000 acres of Caernarfonshire alone, with 618 farms and 873 cottages in the county. 3,000 men were employed at the quarry, by far the largest such concern in the world. Today, covering 3,500 acres and worked to a depth of 1,500 feet, the quarry is still the largest 'hand-made' hole in the earth's surface.

Throughout the 19th century the estate, and the quarry in particular, continued to be the engine for economic development in the region, stimulating the growth of both Port Penrhyn and the city of Bangor. Roads, schools, houses and cottages, churches and recreation grounds were built on estate land, and often at the landlord's expense, since the income, from quarrying at least, continued to be more than ample. Like the other great estates, it fulfilled many of the functions that were to become, after the 1888 Local Government Act, those of the county councils. After that time, parliamentary reform, agricultural depression, the growth of organised labour and the rise of local administration all combined to diminish the influence of the Penrhyn Estate and its owners.

'It is but justice to the successor of the late Lord Penrhyn to say that, along with the estate, he appears to inherit the same spirit for improvement', wrote the anonymous author of *The Cambrian Tourist* in 1828, and when Dawkins-Pennant took over the estate on the death of the Dowager Lady Penrhyn in 1816, one of his first acts was to agree with his chief rival in slate production, Thomas Assheton Smith of Vaynol, a system of common prices that would avoid the limiting effects of a price war and clear the way for further expansion. Assheton Smith's Dinorwic quarries remained a close second to Penrhyn for the rest of the century, and between them they dominated the industry. The Penrhyn quarry produced 40,000 tons of slate in 1820, employing 1,000 men, and growth accelerated over the next twenty years (especially after the repeal in 1831 of Pitt's wartime slate duty), under the management of James Wyatt, thirteenth child of Benjamin, whom he succeeded as general agent in 1817.

In the course of this period, the settlement that came to be known as Bethesda, close to the quarry, expanded from the first building, in 1820, of the Independent chapel of that name. Slate was the material of the moment. The building journals carried recommendations for its use not merely on the roofs of the ever-growing cities but for fireplaces, table tops, 'fittings-up of offices or living rooms, coffee-houses, and public houses', 'panels of doors and window shutters, shelves of every sort … fire proofing'. New workers' housing had to be built at Moel y Ci, and improvements were needed at Port Penrhyn. In 1820 Dawkins-Pennant set up a new cast-iron bridge over the Cegin so that the tramway could pass right on to the wharf, which he extended in 1827–30.

The Jamaican estates were less prosperous during the first half of the century. The dismissal of an attorney for corruption in Lady Penrhyn's time was followed by a series of stormy seasons and low yields, and in 1833 all British slaves were emancipated. But Dawkins-Pennant's main preoccupation for most of his life at Penrhyn was the construction of his new castle, and so he entrusted the aggrandisement of the estate to his son-in-law and successor.

Soon after succeeding, in 1841 Col. Douglas-Pennant had James Wyatt issue an address, printed in English and Welsh, to all his tenants, which is remarkable in revealing how much of the land was still in cultivation as opposed to pasture. Wyatt wrote that the tenantry were on a ruinous course of exhaustive cropping, shallow ploughing, and poor husbandry of hay and pasture, and were able to raise less stock, which in turn yielded less manure. Large-scale improvements by the landlord were also needed. 'Col. Pennant's wish is to see his Property improved', he concluded, 'and, under a better system of husbandry, a thriving and improving class of Farmers. It is impossible, in the present advancing state of society, that he can willingly suffer his Farms to continue in their present neglected and ill-arranged condition.'

Old farmhouses and buildings were rapidly replaced with new ones to the agent's own designs, and in 1847 Col. Douglas-Pennant began the enlargement of the estate by accepting the mortgage of Lord Mostyn's lands in the parishes of Ysbyty Ifan and Penmachno near Betws-y-Coed. In 1854 the mortgages were transferred, and in the following year the adjacent land of the former Vaughan estate of Pant Glas was also acquired from Lord Mostyn. This was sporting as well as agricultural land, including the vast moorland expanse known as the Migneint near the source of the Conwy, and it was for sporting purposes that Col. Douglas-Pennant bought the nearby villa of Glan Conway, and Dinas, the house formerly used by Thomas Telford as a base for the building of the long inclined stretch of the Holyhead road south of Betws-y-Coed. During shooting, young ladies and married couples would stay at Glan Conway, and the young men at Dinas, from where a pony and trap would bring them to Glan Conway after breakfast. The villages of Ysbyty Ifan and Penmachno preserve

many examples of the 'vernacular revival' buildings put up by the estate in the 1850s, and both parish churches were rebuilt around 1860, somewhat regrettably in the case of Penmachno.

By the early 1870s the estate stood at 41,348 acres in Caernarfonshire, 5,377 at Wicken in Northamptonshire, 121 in Kent and 77 in Buckinghamshire, yielding £71,000 per annum. Of this rent roll, the £63,000 that came from Caernarfonshire farms was not as handsome as it seemed. 'There is not much encouragement to purchase land in Caernarvonshire whatever the nominal rent may be', wrote the 1st Lord Penrhyn in 1872. 'I find that as soon as it comes into my possession the calls on me for immediate repairs, new buildings, drainage, enclosure, churches, schools, Parsonage houses, and stipends for incompetent incumbents equal if they do not exceed the total nominal rent.'

The mainstay of the 1st Lord Penrhyn's income was the quarry, which in 1859 produced 120,000 tons, giving a net annual income of £100,000, and the port was again extended and deepened in 1855. With 2,500 men employed, it was no longer practicable to manage the quarry as part of the estate, and when James Wyatt retired in 1860, the posts of estate agent and quarry manager became separate.

The Penrhyn Slate Quarry in 1832; painted by Henry Hawkins

The Great Strike

Lord Penrhyn was dismayed when, in 1865, the quarrymen began to form themselves into a union. Concerned that his traditional paternalistic approach was being threatened by the emergence of an intermediary body, he quickly saw to its disbandment. However, in the next ten years the movement towards organisation grew, and in 1874, the year in which steam locomotives were first introduced on a new railway to the port, the North Wales Quarrymen's Union was officially formed, with the immediate support of more than half the employees in the region. After a brief strike its role was recognised at the Penrhyn quarry by the Pennant Lloyd Agreement, named after Lord Penrhyn's agent. Both Lord Penrhyn and his heir George Sholto were recovering from illness at the time. Later, Adela Douglas-Pennant wrote that, had they been fully involved, a firmer line would have been taken, but 'sooner or later the wave of trades unionism Surging over the land must have swept into the quarry'.

The firm line was adopted by George Sholto when he took over the quarry business in 1885, a year before succeeding as 2nd Baron. Profits had declined since 1874, which he attributed entirely to the influence of the union and their committee. He revoked the Pennant Lloyd Agrement with the words 'I decline altogether to sanction the interference of anybody (corporate or individual) between employer and employed in the working of the Quarry'.

The next decade was characterised by increasing antagonism between the Quarrymen's Committee and the management, culminating in the

(Right) Workers are escorted back to the quarry by the police. From the radical Welsh weekly Papur Pawb*, 15 June 1901*

first major strike, in 1896–7. The Penrhyn quarry had become a focus of attention from all quarters. There was an angry debate in the House of Commons, and Lloyd George made a speech at Carmarthen, denouncing Lord Penrhyn. But this dispute, settled without major concessions on the employer's part, was but the prelude to what has become a legendary episode in industrial history, the strike of 1900–3.

Growing resentment against individual contractors employed in the quarry flared up one afternoon in October 1900, when a serious riot took place on one of the galleries. Twenty-six men were prosecuted, and Lloyd George acted in their defence in court. Six were convicted and dismissed, but on 22 November, the day the remaining twenty returned to the quarry, the entire workforce walked out, and after negotiations with Lord Penrhyn's manager,

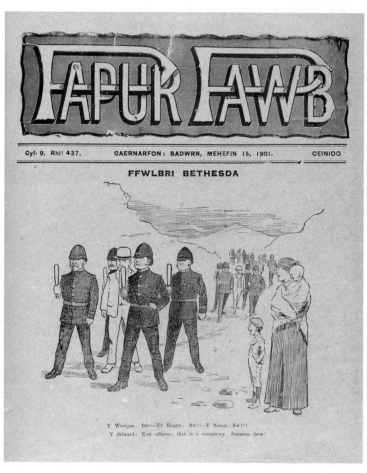

E.A. Young, broke down, went on strike. As the strike developed, the key question became the recognition of the union as an intermediary body between the managers and employees. When the quarry reopened in June 1901, 400 men returned to work, but antagonism grew between them and the majority who remained out. Their strike pay was modest, and although large contributions came in from the TUC and appeals in the national press and the TUC, many were forced to seek work in the South Wales coal-mines. When their leader, W.J. Parry, was successfully sued for libel against Lord Penrhyn, his costs were met from a public appeal, and three local choirs toured Britain to raise money for the strikers. At holiday times, when those who had left returned to their families, there was often violence, which necessitated the drafting of extra police and troops.

When the press and the TUC ended their support in 1903, the strike began to collapse, and in November there was a vote in favour of a return to work. The strike ended at a time of general depression in the slate industry, and years of hardship and bitterness followed for those who did not find a place in the reduced workforce.

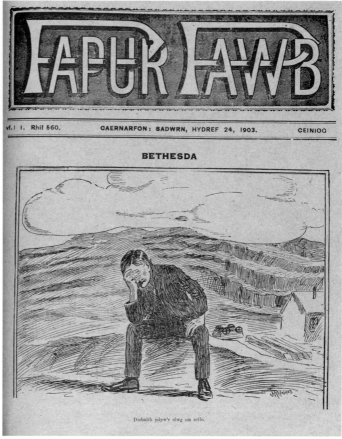

A quarryman in despair at the continued failure to reach a settlement. From Papur Pawb, *24 October 1903*

Retrenchment

On the estate at large, there had been acquisitions and heavy expenditure in improvements and new buildings (a total of £175,000 between 1867 and 1892), but rents had not risen for many years, and in 1893 the rental income from 72,000 acres had declined to £21,000.

The end of the Great Strike in 1903 coincided with a slump in the building industry, and by the time the First World War broke out, production at the quarry was half that achieved in 1898. When building surged after 1918, foreign competitors and home-produced tiles inflicted

further damage. Edward Sholto, 3rd Lord Penrhyn, presided, from his main seat at Wicken, over a period of retrenchment and sales, and his son Hugh Napier, 4th Baron, disposed of Richard Pennant's Royal Hotel at Capel Curig, and all the Jamaican property by 1940.

After his death in 1949, the greater part of the estate with Penrhyn Castle passed via the Inland Revenue to the National Trust, and is still managed as over 40,000 acres of mountain and upland pasture, supporting over 60 farms.

In 2007 the quarry was acquired from Sir Alfred McAlpine Ltd by LBS, a Belfast-based building products company which is planning to make a substantial investment to ensure the future of the quarry and its 300 employees.

The Families of Penrhyn

Asterisk denotes portrait in the house

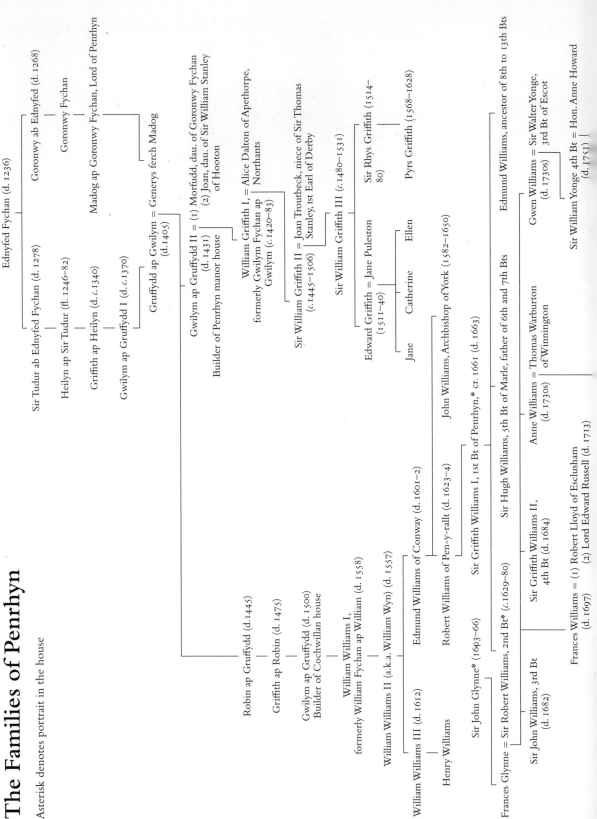

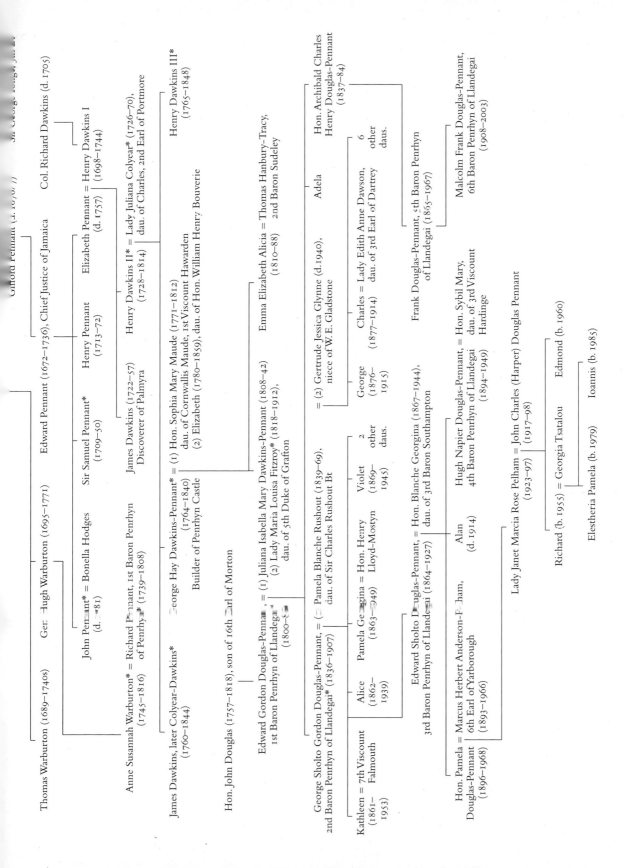

Thomas Warburton (1689–1740s)

Ger... Hugh Warburton (1695–1771)

Gifford Pennant (d. 1670/1)   Sir George Long, jurist

Edward Pennant (1672–1736), Chief Justice of Jamaica

Col. Richard Dawkins (d. 1705)

John Pennant* = Bonella Hodges
(d. ...81)

Henry Pennant
(1713–72)

Elizabeth Pennant = Henry Dawkins I
(d. 1757)   (1698–1744)

Sir Samuel Pennant*
(1709–50)

Anne Susannah Warburton* = Richard Pennant, 1st Baron Penrhyn
(1745–1816)   of Penrhyn* (1739–1808)

James Dawkins (1722–57)
Discoverer of Palmyra

Henry Dawkins II* = Lady Juliana Colyear* (1726–70),
(1728–1814)   dau. of Charles, 2nd Earl of Portmore

Henry Dawkins III*
(1765–1848)

James Dawkins, later Colyear-Dawkins*
(1760–1844)

George Hay Dawkins-Pennant* = (1) Hon. Sophia Mary Maude (1771–1812),
(1764–1840)   dau. of Cornwallis Maude, 1st Viscount Hawarden
Builder of Penrhyn Castle   (2) Elizabeth (1780–1859), dau. of Hon. William Henry Bouverie

Hon. John Douglas (1757–1818), son of 16th Earl of Morton

Emma Elizabeth Alicia = Thomas Hanbury-Tracy,
(1810–88)   2nd Baron Sudeley

Hon. Archibald Charles
Henry Douglas-Pennant
(1837–84)

Edward Gordon Douglas-Pennant, = (1) Juliana Isabella Mary Dawkins-Pennant (1808–42)
1st Baron Penrhyn of Llandegai*   (2) Lady Maria Louisa Fitzroy* (1818–1912),
(1800–8...   dau. of 5th Duke of Grafton

Adela

= (2) Gertrude Jessica Glynne (d. 1940),
niece of W. E. Gladstone

6
other
daus.

George Sholto Gordon Douglas-Pennant, = (= Pamela Blanche Rushout (1839–69),
2nd Baron Penrhyn of Llandegai* (1836–1907)   dau. of Sir Charles Rushout Bt

George
(1876–
1915)

Charles = Lady Edith Anne Dawson,
(1877–1914)   dau. of 3rd Earl of Dartrey

Frank Douglas-Pennant, 5th Baron Penrhyn
of Llandegai (1865–1967)

Malcolm Frank Douglas-Pennant,
6th Baron Penrhyn of Llandegai
(1908–2003)

Kathleen = 7th Viscount
(1861–   Falmouth
1953)

Alice
(1862–
1939)

Pamela Georgina = Hon. Henry
(1863–1949)   Lloyd-Mostyn

Violet
(1869–
1945)

2
other
daus.

Edward Sholto Douglas-Pennant, = Hon. Blanche Georgina (1867–1944),
3rd Baron Penrhyn of Llandegai (1864–1927)   dau. of 3rd Baron Southampton

Hugh Napier Douglas-Pennant, = Hon. Sybil Mary,
4th Baron Penrhyn of Llandegai   dau. of 3rd Viscount
(1894–1949)   Hardinge

Hon. Pamela = Marcus Herbert Anderson-Pelham,
Douglas-Pennant   6th Earl of Yarborough
(1896–1968)   (1893–1966)

Alan
(d. 1914)

Lady Janet Marcia Rose Pelham = John Charles (Harper) Douglas Pennant
(1923–97)   (1917–98)

Richard (b. 1955) = Georgia Tsatalou

Edmond (b. 1960)

Elestheria Pamela (b. 1979)

Ioannis (b. 1985)

Bibliography

Manuscript sources

The Penrhyn Castle MSS, comprising 9,000 items from 1288 to 1949, are deposited in the archive of University College, North Wales, Bangor. The papers of the Penrhyn Quarry are on deposit in the Gwynedd Record Office, Caernarfon.

Early descriptions of Penrhyn

Anon., *The Cambrian Tourist; or Post-chaise companion through Wales*, 1828.

Bingley, Rev. W., *A Tour round North Wales performed during the Summer of 1798*, 2 vols, 1800.

Bingley, Rev. W., *Excursions in North Wales*, 3rd edition, by his son W. R. Bingley, 1838.

Costello, Louise Stuart, *The Falls, Lakes and Mountains of North Wales*, 1845.

Evans, Rev. J., *The Beauties of England and Wales*, xxiv, 1809–12.

Hall, Edward Hyde, 'A Description of Caernarvonshire (1809–1811)', *Caernarvonshire Historical Society Record Series*, No. 2, 1952.

Llwyd, Angharad, *A History of the Island of Mona or Anglesey*, 1833.

Llwyd, Richard, 'The History of Wales', revised and corrected with 'Topographical Notices', 1832.

Parry, John ('Bardd Alaw'), *A Trip to North Wales made in 1839*, 1839.

Pennant, Thomas, *Tours in Wales*, 1778–81, 1st collected edn, 3 vols, 1810.

Pückler-Muskau, Prince Herman Ludwig Heinrich von, *Tour in England, Ireland and France in the years 1826–1829*, 4 vols, 1832.

Rodenberg, Julius, *An Autumn in Wales* (1856), 1858, trans., and ed. W. Linnard.

Sinclair, Catherine, *Hill and Valley, or Wales and the Welsh*, 1839 [based on a journey in June–August 1833].

Williams, William, *Observations on the Snowdon Mountains*, 1802.

Williams, William, 'A Survey of the Ancient and Present state of the County of Caernarfon', by 'A Land Surveyor', 1806, *Trans. Caernarvonshire Historical Society*, xxxiii, xxxiv, xxxvi, 1972–5.

General

Douglas-Pennant, Hon. Adela, *A Short Summary of the life of Edward Gordon Douglas, 1st Lord Penrhyn, compiled by his youngest daughter Adela*, 1910–12 [unpublished transcript].

Douglas-Pennant, Hon. Alice, *Catalogue of the Pictures at Penrhyn Castle and Mortimer House in 1901*, 1902.

Douglas-Pennant, E. H., *The Pennants of Penrhyn*, 1982.

Douglas-Pennant, E. H., *The Welsh Families of Penrhyn*, 1985.

Ellis-Jones, Peter, 'The Wyatts of Lime Grove, Llandegai', *Trans. Caernarvonshire Historical Society*, xlii, 1981.

Hague, Douglas B., 'Penrhyn Castle, Caernarvon – I', *Country Life*, cxviii, 14 July 1955.

Hague, Douglas B., 'Penrhyn Castle', *Trans. Caernarvonshire Historical Society*, xx, 1959.

Haslam, Richard, 'Penrhyn Castle, Gwynedd – I and II', *Country Life*, clxxxi, 29 Oct., 5 Nov. 1987.

Hussey, Christopher, 'Penrhyn Castle, Caernarvon – II and III', *Country Life*, cxviii, 21 and 28 July 1955; reprinted in *English Country Houses: Late Georgian*, 1958, pp. 181–92.

Lindsay, Jean, *A History of the North Wales Slate Industry*, David & Charles, 1974.

Lindsay, Jean, 'The Pennants and Jamaica, 1665– 1800', I and II, *Trans. Caernarvonshire Historical Society*, 1982 and 1983.

Lindsay, Jean, *The Great Strike*, 1987.

Linnard, W., 'Angus Duncan Webster: A Scottish forester at Penrhyn Castle, North Wales', *Scottish Forestry*, 1985, pp. 265–74.

Mowl, Timothy, 'The Norman Revival in British Architecture 1790–1870', PhD, Oxford Univ., 1981.

Sales, John, 'Victorian grandeur revived: gardens of Penrhyn Castle, Bangor, Gwynedd', *Country Life*, 31 October 1985.

Wyatt, Lewis William, *A Collection of Architectural Designs… Executed in a Variety of Buildings upon the Estates of the Right Hon. Lord Penrhyn*, 1800–1.